# THE
# LOVING
# KITCHEN

# THE
# LOVING
# KITCHEN

DOWNRIGHT DELICIOUS SOUTHERN
RECIPES TO SHARE WITH
FAMILY, FRIENDS, AND NEIGHBORS

# LEANN RICE

NELSON
BOOKS

An Imprint of Thomas Nelson

Published in Nashville, Tennessee, by Nelson Books, an imprint of Thomas Nelson. Nelson Books and Thomas Nelson are registered trademarks of HarperCollins Christian Publishing, Inc.

Published in association with Wheelhouse Literary Group

Thomas Nelson, Inc., titles may be purchased in bulk for educational, business, fund-raising, or sales promotional use. For information, please e-mail SpecialMarkets@ThomasNelson.com.

Unless otherwise noted, Scripture quotations are taken from the Holy Bible, New International Version®, NIV®. Copyright © 1973, 1978, 1984, 2011 by Biblica, Inc.™ Used by permission of Zondervan. All rights reserved worldwide. www.zondervan.com

Scripture quotations marked NLT are from the Holy Bible, New Living Translation. © 1996. Used by permission of Tyndale House Publishers, Inc., Wheaton, Illinois 60189. All rights reserved.

Page 78: Photography by Mark Boughton and food and prop styling by Teresa Blackburn

Pages 74 and 150: Photos from Shutterstock.com

Library of Congress Cataloging-in-Publication Data

Rice, LeAnn, 1964–
   The loving kitchen : downright delicious Southern recipes to share with family, friends, and neighbors / LeAnn Rice.
       pages cm
   Includes bibliographical references and index.
   ISBN 978-1-4016-0526-1 (paperback : alkaline paper) 1. Cooking, American—Southern style. 2. Sharing. I. Title.
   TX715.2.S68R49 2014
   641.5975—dc23                                                                                  2013043403

Printed in the United States of America

14 15 16 17 18 RRD 6 5 4 3 2 1

## FOR NICK

You fill my life with more love and more joy
than my heart could ever contain.

# CONTENTS

When Christ said, "I was hungry and you fed me,"
He didn't mean only the hunger for bread and
food; He also meant the hunger to be loved.

—MOTHER TERESA

# INTRODUCTION: WELCOME TO MY TABLE

The kitchen table is a place where memories are made and cherished for years to come. It's a place to connect with those we love—to encourage and support one another and to celebrate the many blessings in our lives. Gathering around the table provides the opportunity to share life with those we hold dear.

But life seems to go by too quickly, each day moving a little faster than the one before. We spend more time eating on the go than we spend sitting down together to share a home-cooked meal. I want us to slow down and return to the heart of the home—the family table—and to keep a place at our table open so we may invite others in.

*The Loving Kitchen* is my way of inviting you to my table.

Wouldn't it be wonderful if we actually could fit around my kitchen table? All of us. At the same time. We would share recipes, encourage one another, laugh together, shed tears together, compare kitchen disaster stories (we all have them), and create lifelong memories.

And we would share food.

And swap pound cake recipes.

So much of life happens in the kitchen. Some of my most cherished memories are of gathering around a large table filled with food. In fact, most memories of my paternal grandmother revolve around her kitchen.

We lived several hundred miles away from Nanny and Grandfather, so we only saw them a couple of times a year. After a ten-hour drive, we arrived to a table filled with food. Nanny spent the entire day in her kitchen, making five entrées so each of us had our favorite. Food was love, and she expressed her love for us by preparing and serving our favorite meals.

This act of love was not lost on me. Nor was how special it made me feel to know Nanny loved me that much. And I especially remember the look of joy on her face as I sighed with that first bite of scrumptious love.

Loving others through food is not a new concept. Throughout time, God has prompted people to use food as a means of reaching out to others to meet their needs. Jesus Himself nourished five thousand hungry listeners with some fish and barley loaves on a hillside.

Good food has always been a way not only to nourish but to thank, encourage, console, serve, celebrate, and ultimately love.

Welcoming your son home with his favorite dinner after he struck out at his baseball game . . .

Bringing a basket filled with warm muffins to coworkers during a stressful workweek . . .

Inviting a lonely neighbor to your table for a home-cooked meal . . .

Delivering a simple, comforting casserole to a family experiencing a loss . . .

Or creating an elaborate cake to celebrate a special occasion or to make an ordinary day extraordinary . . .

Extending hospitality, simply or extravagantly, is a tangible way to express your love to family, friends, neighbors, coworkers, and strangers. It's a way to show others they have not gone unnoticed, that they matter.

Friends, I pray the recipes and glimpses into my heart you now hold in your hands will be a blessing to you.

I pray your eyes are open to the world around you and you will invite the hungry, the lost, and the hurting to your table, extending mercy and grace to "the least of these" (Matt. 25:40).

I pray you experience His grace and His love every moment of every day.

I pray your hearts are happy.

I pray your tummies are full.

Welcome. I've set a place for you at my table.

Love and blessings,
LeAnn

# NOTES AND TIPS FROM MY KITCHEN TO YOURS

Because I have such a deep-rooted love of cooking, it seemed natural to pursue some type of career in the food industry. While I did try my hand at catering, I quickly discovered cooking for strangers was not the same as cooking for those I love. I am not a professional chef with years of training in culinary arts. I'm simply a gal who loves to make people happy by cooking for and serving them from my heart.

My kitchen is simple. It's an ordinary kitchen with ordinary tools and utensils, ordinary appliances, and ordinary ingredients. I don't own any professional equipment, and I don't shop in specialty food stores. You will be able to make any recipe in this book using hand-me-down pots and pans and ingredients found in your local grocery store. And while some of my recipes have an extra step or two, none are complicated.

Whether you are a seasoned home cook or taking your first steps into the kitchen, we all have room to grow, new things to learn, and cooking traditions to begin. Throughout this book I share some of the lessons I've learned through my own adventures—and disasters—in the kitchen. I've also listed general notes and tips here for easy reference.

- Read the entire recipe before you begin so there aren't any surprises after you've already started.
- Dry the surface of meat and poultry before browning. Too much moisture will cause the meat to steam instead of brown.
- Place raw bacon and boneless pieces of meat in the freezer for 15 minutes to make them easier to slice.
- Unless otherwise noted, when sugar is listed among the ingredients, I am referring to white granulated sugar.
- If a recipe calls for buttermilk and you don't have it on hand, you can make sour milk as a replacement. Simply add one tablespoon of fresh lemon juice or white vinegar to a 1-cup measuring cup. Fill the cup with milk and let it sit for ten minutes.

- When a recipe calls for eggs, always crack them into a separate container before adding them to the rest of the ingredients. It's a lot easier to remove a broken piece of eggshell if it's not hiding in the cake batter. The easiest way to remove a piece of eggshell is to use another, larger piece of eggshell. The pieces are drawn together, so the little broken piece will cling to the larger shell, making it easier to remove.
- Always preheat your oven as directed before placing the food inside.
- For prettier cupcakes, line your muffin tins with a double layer of decorative liners. Paper baking cups absorb some of the oils from the batter, which dulls the color and design. When you add the second layer, the inner layer will absorb the oils, leaving the outer layer sharp and vibrant.
- When cooking pasta, always cook for one minute less than directed on the package, and if the pasta will be served coated in a sauce, always reserve 1 cup of the pasta water before straining. Add about 1/4 cup to your sauce, then toss with the pasta. You can add more if the pasta seems too heavy. The reserved starchy water loosens the sauce and helps it cling to the pasta. This tip also works with pasta casseroles. If it seems too heavy, just stir in a little pasta water.
- Don't add oil to the pasta water to keep pasta from sticking together. If you use a large pot with plenty of water, your pasta will move around as it boils and will not stick together. Adding oil will only keep the sauce from clinging to cooked pasta.
- Whenever possible, use local, in-season ingredients. Your ingredients will always be at their peak, and you will be supporting local farmers.

And two final tips . . .

- Don't strive for perfection, and don't be afraid of making mistakes. Remember, it's about the heart, not the technique. If your cheesecake cracks, cover it with whipped cream. If your mashed potatoes are runny, turn them into loaded baked potato soup. If your omelet falls apart, tell everyone you made extra-special scrambled eggs. And if the entire dinner bursts into flames . . . order pizza.
- Cook from your heart. You can take ordinary ingredients and make something extraordinary when you add love. It really is as simple as that. The goal isn't to make food that is complicated. The goal is to get everyone back to the table, together, and to extend love and grace through a meal made from the heart.

# MORNING FARE

*Nobody can go back and start a new beginning,
but anyone can start today and make a new ending.*
—MARIA ROBINSON

A satisfying, well-balanced breakfast gives us energy to make the most of our day, but on hurried weekday mornings, my family struggles to find enough time to sit down for a bowl of cereal.

When Nick was in elementary school, I made him a peanut butter sandwich with frozen whole grain waffles almost every morning. It was fast, healthier than toaster pastries, and he could eat in the car on the way to school. Oh, how I wish I had slowed down and taken more time to encourage him before running out the door to face whatever the day before us held.

Sweet conversations over perfectly crisp bacon and fluffy pancakes dripping with melted butter and pure maple syrup are usually reserved for weekends. But what if we took just one weekday morning and actually planned family breakfast? It doesn't have to be elaborate. You don't have to wake up at 4:00 a.m. to get started. In fact, you will find several make-ahead breakfasts in this section. Make family breakfast something everyone looks forward to. Just one extra day a week. One.

## FROM THE OVEN

Overnight Breakfast Casserole

Baked Eggs in a Cradle

Roasted Breakfast Potatoes and Bacon

Sugared Bacon

Ham and Egg Enchiladas

Almond-Coconut Granola

Baked Fruit

Baked Oatmeal

## FROM THE GRIDDLE

Peanut Butter and Jelly French Toast

Eggnog French Toast

Buttermilk Pancakes

Pumpkin Spice Pancakes

## FROM THE SKILLET

Maple-Glazed Breakfast Sausage

Grilled Bacon, Egg, and Cheese Sandwich

Swedish Pancakes

# OVERNIGHT BREAKFAST CASSEROLE

*Special mornings should be spent with those you love, not laboring in the kitchen, so I love a dish that can be prepared the night before. This easy casserole is one of my absolute favorites. The aroma of cinnamon will fill your home and beckon family and overnight guests to the breakfast table.*

**MAKES 8 SERVINGS.**

1 (16-ounce) loaf cinnamon swirl or brown sugar cinnamon bread, cut into 1-inch cubes

1 (12-ounce) package maple sausage links, cooked and cut into bite-size pieces

6 large eggs

2 cups half-and-half

1 cup milk

2 teaspoons vanilla extract

¾ teaspoon ground cinnamon

¼ teaspoon ground nutmeg

½ cup (1 stick) butter, softened

1 cup firmly packed light brown sugar

2 tablespoons pure maple syrup, plus more for serving

1 cup chopped pecans

Confectioners' sugar for serving

Spray a 2-quart casserole dish with nonstick cooking spray. Arrange bread cubes in bottom of baking dish and top with sausage.

In a medium bowl whisk together the eggs, half-and-half, milk, vanilla, cinnamon, and nutmeg, and pour over bread and sausage in the casserole dish. Cover tightly with aluminum foil or plastic wrap and refrigerate overnight.

In the morning, preheat the oven to 350 degrees and uncover the casserole.

In a small bowl stir the butter, brown sugar, maple syrup, and pecans together and drop by the spoonful all over the top of casserole. Bake for 40 to 50 minutes or until the center of the casserole is set. Remove from the oven and let sit for 15 minutes.

Serve with a drizzle of maple syrup and a dusting of confectioners' sugar . . . not because it needs it, but just because it looks pretty!

*Each new day is a chance to make a new beginning. A chance to count our blessings. A chance to show kindness, extend forgiveness, and love with all our hearts.*

# BAKED EGGS IN A CRADLE

*Baking eggs is a great way to cook several eggs at the same time, and they make a beautiful presentation. Try baking them in hollowed-out peppers or in muffin tins lined with Canadian bacon or prosciutto.*

**MAKES 1 SERVING.**

1 large crusty dinner roll or mini brioche

1 tablespoon butter, melted

1 large egg

1 teaspoon heavy cream

Salt and black pepper to taste

Scant teaspoon chopped fresh chives or parsley

1 tablespoon shredded or grated Parmesan cheese

Preheat oven to 350 degrees. Slice the top off the roll or brioche, and carefully remove enough bread from the bottom portion of the roll until you have it hollowed out enough to hold the egg. Place on a cookie sheet.

Brush the inside of the hollowed-out roll and the cut side of the top that was removed with melted butter. Crack the egg into the hollow. Add cream and sprinkle with salt and pepper, herbs, and Parmesan cheese.

Bake for 10 minutes, and then place the top half of roll on the cookie sheet, cut side up. Bake an additional 10 minutes or until egg is set and bread is golden. Remove from the oven and place the top onto the roll or tilt to the side. Serve immediately.

# ROASTED BREAKFAST POTATOES AND BACON

*As the bacon cooks, the grease flavors the potatoes and onions. There really is nothing more to say, is there?*

---

**MAKES 6 SERVINGS.**

3 large russet potatoes, cut into 1-inch cubes

1 small onion, chopped

1 tablespoon olive oil

1 teaspoon salt

½ teaspoon black pepper

12 slices bacon

Preheat the oven to 400 degrees. Spray a 15 x 10-inch jelly-roll pan with nonstick cooking spray.

In a large bowl combine the potatoes and onion. Drizzle with olive oil and sprinkle with salt and pepper. Arrange bacon slices around the edge of the jelly-roll pan, and then arrange potatoes and onions in a single layer in the center of the pan.

Bake for 20 minutes. Turn the bacon slices over and stir the potatoes. Continue baking for 20 to 25 minutes or until bacon is crispy and potatoes are tender and golden.

# SUGARED BACON

*Oh my! This stuff is like candy. Please make double or triple the amount you think you need. Trust me on this.*

---

**MAKES 4 TO 6 SERVINGS. (WHO AM I KIDDING . . . YOU'LL BE LUCKY IF IT SERVES 2!)**

1 cup firmly packed light brown sugar

1 pound center-cut sliced bacon

Place oven rack one position above the center. Preheat the oven to 400 degrees.

Line a 15 x 10-inch jelly-roll pan with foil. Place a large rack on the lined jelly-roll pan and spray with nonstick cooking spray.

Spread brown sugar on the bottom of a shallow dish. Coat each strip of bacon by laying it in the brown sugar and turning it over, pressing sugar into each side. Arrange on the rack.

Bake for 20 to 25 minutes or until bacon is crisp.

# HAM AND EGG ENCHILADAS

*This breakfast casserole is very easy and very filling. You assemble it the night before, then cover and refrigerate it overnight before baking it in the morning. It's also very delicious!*

**MAKES 6 SERVINGS.**

8 (8-inch) flour tortillas

2 cups cubed cooked ham

3 green onions, sliced

3 cups shredded Cheddar cheese, divided

6 large eggs

2 cups half-and-half

1 tablespoon all-purpose flour

1 (4.5-ounce) can mild chopped green chilies

¼ teaspoon salt

¼ teaspoon black pepper

Salsa for serving, optional

Spray a 9 x 13-inch casserole dish with nonstick cooking spray.

Lay each tortilla on a clean countertop or on a cutting board. Divide the ham and green onions among the 8 tortillas. Top each with 2 to 3 tablespoons of Cheddar. Roll up the tortillas and place them seam side down in the casserole dish.

In a large bowl beat the eggs and then whisk in half-and-half, flour, chilies, salt, and pepper. Pour over the tortillas. Cover and refrigerate overnight.

Remove from the refrigerator about a half hour before baking. Preheat the oven to 350 degrees.

Bake covered for 30 minutes. Uncover and top with remaining cheese. Return to the oven and continue baking uncovered for 15 to 20 minutes or until cheese is melted. Remove from the oven and let stand for 15 minutes to set up. Serve with salsa (if desired).

# ALMOND-COCONUT GRANOLA

*This homemade granola has just a touch of sweetness. It's a yummy (and quite addictive) snack on its own, and it stays crunchy in milk. Use it to make yogurt parfaits by layering it with fresh fruit and yogurt, or sprinkle on baked fruit for a crunchy topping.*

**MAKES 5 CUPS.**

¼ cup (½ stick) butter, melted
¼ cup honey
¼ cup firmly packed brown sugar
½ teaspoon ground cinnamon
2 cups rolled oats
1 cup sliced almonds
1 cup flaked coconut
1 cup raisins or dried cranberries

Preheat the oven to 325 degrees. Spray a 15 x 10-inch jelly-roll pan with nonstick cooking spray.

In a small bowl mix the melted butter and honey. In another small bowl combine the brown sugar and cinnamon. In a large, shallow bowl combine the rolled oats and almonds. Pour the butter mixture over the oat mixture and stir to mix well. Sprinkle with the brown sugar and cinnamon and stir to coat well. Spread in a single layer on the jelly-roll pan.

Bake for 15 minutes. Remove from the oven and mix in the coconut. Return to oven and bake until golden, approximately 5 to 10 minutes. Remove from the oven and stir in the raisins or cranberries. Cool completely, stirring occasionally. The granola will crisp as it cools. Store in an airtight container.

# BAKED FRUIT

*You can use any combination of fruit in this dish. Top it with homemade granola and serve it as part of a brunch buffet.*

---

**MAKES 8 SERVINGS.**

4 apples, peeled and cut into thin wedges

2 pears, peeled and cut into thin wedges

2 cups raspberries, blackberries, or blueberries (or any combination)

⅔ cup firmly packed light brown sugar

2 tablespoons all-purpose flour

1 teaspoon ground cinnamon

¼ teaspoon ground allspice

⅛ teaspoon ground cloves

6 tablespoons butter, melted

Almond-Coconut Granola (recipe on page 9)

Preheat the oven to 350 degrees. Spray a 9 x 13-inch casserole dish with nonstick cooking spray.

Combine the apples, pears, and berries in a large bowl.

In a medium bowl whisk together the brown sugar, flour, cinnamon, allspice, and cloves. Stir in the melted butter, pour mixture over the fruit, and toss to coat. Transfer to the casserole dish.

Cover the dish with foil and bake for 30 minutes. Remove foil and continue baking for 30 minutes or until fruit is tender. Remove from the oven and let sit for 15 minutes. Top with Almond-Coconut Granola right before serving.

# BAKED OATMEAL

*Baked oatmeal is the perfect breakfast any day, but especially on cold winter mornings. It reheats well in the microwave, so it's a great dish to make on Sunday to serve throughout the week when you don't have as much time to prepare a nutritious breakfast. It will warm your tummy!*

**MAKES 6 TO 8 SERVINGS.**

¼ cup (½ stick) butter, plus extra for preparing pan

4 cups milk

½ cup firmly packed light brown sugar

1 teaspoon ground cinnamon

Dash or two of ground nutmeg

1 teaspoon salt

2 cups old-fashioned rolled oats

1 cup chopped apples

1 cup raisins

1 cup chopped almonds

Pure maple syrup for serving

Preheat oven to 350 degrees. Butter a 2-quart casserole dish.

Combine butter, milk, brown sugar, cinnamon, nutmeg, and salt in a saucepan and bring to a boil over medium-high heat. Stir often to keep from scorching. As soon as the mixture comes to a boil, remove from heat.

In a large bowl combine oats, apples, raisins, and almonds. Pour the hot milk mixture over the oat mixture and stir to combine. Pour into the casserole dish. Bake uncovered for 35 minutes.

Spoon servings into bowls, and then drizzle with maple syrup so the oatmeal sits in a little pool of maple goodness.

NOTE: If it's a special occasion and you aren't concerned about the extra calories and sugar, dot the top with butter and then sprinkle with a little brown sugar and cinnamon. The baked oatmeal is absolutely delicious without this extra step, but it does make a lovely presentation when you are serving guests.

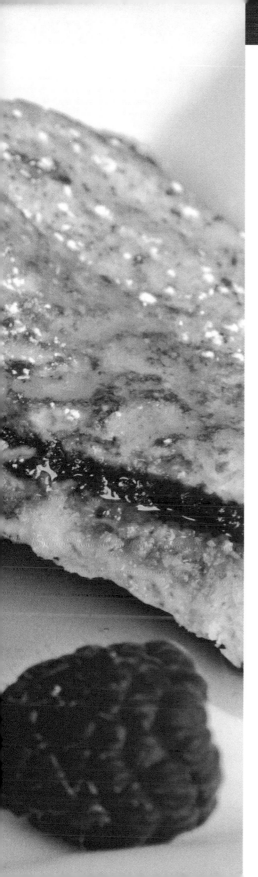

# PEANUT BUTTER AND JELLY FRENCH TOAST

*I've never met a kid (of any age) who didn't love these. They are delicious! You can use this same technique with different fillings. Try strawberry cream cheese with fresh sliced strawberries or chocolate hazelnut spread with sliced bananas. Pineapple cream cheese with toasted coconut would also make a great combination. Or brie with thinly sliced pears for something a little more savory. My mind is reeling with possibilities!*

**MAKES 4 SERVINGS.**

8 slices sandwich bread
Peanut butter
Favorite flavor jam, preserves, or jelly
3 large eggs, beaten
¼ cup milk
¼ teaspoon vanilla extract
Dash of ground cinnamon
Butter for griddle or skillet
Confectioners' sugar for serving
Pure maple syrup for serving

Spread four slices of bread with peanut butter and four slices with jam. Put together to make four peanut butter and jelly sandwiches.

In a flat dish combine the eggs, milk, vanilla, and cinnamon.

Heat a griddle or skillet over medium heat. Melt enough butter to coat the bottom. Gently place one sandwich in the egg mixture, turning over to coat both sides. Transfer to the griddle or skillet. Repeat with the remaining sandwiches. Cook for approximately 4 minutes per side or until golden brown.

To serve, cut each sandwich in half diagonally into triangles. Sprinkle with confectioners' sugar and serve with a little drizzle of maple syrup.

# EGGNOG FRENCH TOAST

*This is a great recipe for using up any leftover eggnog you may have in the back of your refrigerator after the holidays. Even friends who are not eggnog fans love this French toast. It's easy and delicious, and it kicks up your everyday French toast into something special!*

**MAKES 6 SERVINGS.**

Butter for griddle or skillet

3 large eggs

2 cups eggnog

¼ teaspoon ground cinnamon

¼ teaspoon ground nutmeg

1 pound loaf French bread (not too fresh), sliced into 1-inch thick slices

Confectioners' sugar for serving

Butter for serving

Pure maple syrup for serving

Heat a griddle or skillet over medium heat. Coat the surface with butter.

In a shallow bowl whisk the eggs and then add the eggnog, cinnamon, and nutmeg. Dip the bread slices into the egg mixture and turn to coat (do not let them soak). Carefully transfer the slices to the griddle.

Cook for approximately 3 to 4 minutes per side or until golden brown and cooked through.

Remove to a serving platter and dust with sifted confectioners' sugar. Serve with butter and maple syrup.

# BUTTERMILK PANCAKES

*This is my favorite basic buttermilk pancake recipe. It produces a tender and light pancake. If you use butter on your griddle, you will end up with delightful, crisp, buttery edges. Sometimes I add blueberries, thinly sliced peaches, or crumbled bacon to the uncooked side before flipping the pancakes. I stack three on a plate and top with butter and maple syrup. Then I stare at the wondrous sight of the butter melting into the syrup from the warmth of the pancakes . . . for about two seconds. Then I gobble them up!*

**MAKES 10 TO 12 PANCAKES.**

2 cups all-purpose flour

4 tablespoons sugar

1 teaspoon salt

2 teaspoons baking powder

¼ cup (½ stick) butter, melted

2 cups buttermilk

1 large egg

½ teaspoon vanilla

Butter for griddle, plus extra for serving

Pure maple syrup for serving

Preheat the oven to 200 degrees. Place a cooling rack on top of a cookie sheet and place in the oven.

In a medium bowl combine the flour, sugar, salt, and baking powder with a whisk. In another medium bowl whisk the butter, buttermilk, egg, and vanilla to combine. Stir the egg mixture into the flour mixture until smooth but do not overmix. Let sit for 5 minutes.

Preheat a griddle and melt the butter to generously coat.

Use a ⅓ cup ladle to spoon out the batter onto the buttered griddle. Flip after about 3 minutes, or when bottom is golden and top is beginning to look a little dry. Cook other side for about 2 minutes or until golden. Remove and place on rack in the oven to keep warm while you continue with remaining batter.

Serve warm with butter and maple syrup.

# PUMPKIN SPICE PANCAKES

*I find ways to incorporate pumpkin, apples, and cinnamon into as many recipes as possible during the fall months. The aroma these ingredients create while cooking should be bottled as "man-bait" cologne and dabbed behind the ears.*

**MAKES 12 TO 16 PANCAKES.**

2 cups white wheat or all-purpose flour

2 teaspoons baking powder

1 teaspoon baking soda

3 tablespoons firmly packed brown sugar

2 teaspoons pumpkin pie spice

½ teaspoon salt

1 cup pumpkin puree

1 large egg

3 tablespoons butter, melted, plus extra for cooking

1 ½ cups buttermilk

In a medium bowl combine the flour, baking powder, baking soda, brown sugar, pumpkin pie spice, and salt using a whisk.

In a large bowl combine the pumpkin puree, egg, melted butter, and buttermilk. Stir the flour mixture into the pumpkin mixture. Do not overmix. Set aside to rest for 10 minutes. The batter will puff up and appear spongy.

Heat a griddle or skillet over medium heat and coat with a little bit of butter.

Stir the pancake batter. Use a ⅓ cup ladle to spoon out pancakes onto the preheated griddle. Use the back of the ladle to spread the thick batter out a little. Cook pancakes for 2 to 3 minutes per side or until golden brown.

Serve with butter and syrup or cinnamon or honey butter or confectioners' sugar, or just pile everything on them!

# MAPLE-GLAZED BREAKFAST SAUSAGE

*A simple recipe turns ordinary breakfast sausage into something quite extraordinary. If there were such a thing as sausage-flavored candy, it would taste exactly like this.*

**MAKES 8 TO 12 SERVINGS.**

24 breakfast sausage links cooked as directed

⅓ cup pure maple syrup

⅓ cup firmly packed light brown sugar

1 tablespoon coarse-grain mustard

Dash cayenne pepper, optional

After cooking the sausage, drain on paper towels. Remove the grease from the skillet and place skillet over medium heat. Add maple syrup, brown sugar, mustard, and cayenne to skillet and stir to combine. Place cooked sausage in the glaze and cook, stirring every 60 seconds, over medium heat for 3 to 5 minutes or until the glaze is thickened and it coats the sausages. Serve hot.

# GRILLED BACON, EGG, AND CHEESE SANDWICH

*This yummy, messy sandwich also makes a perfect dinner for busy weeknights. There are a couple of tricks to getting this just right. When cooking the egg, you need to break the yolk and spread it around a bit, then turn the egg over and quickly remove it from the heat so the yolk doesn't cook all the way through. The other key is to put thin slices of cheese on both slices of bread and grill them separately instead of putting them together to form a sandwich.*

**MAKES 1 SERVING.**

Butter, softened for spreading, plus more for cooking the egg

2 slices bread

2 sandwich-size slices of Cheddar cheese

1 large egg

3 to 4 slices cooked crispy bacon

Place a heavy skillet over medium heat. Butter one side of each slice of bread and place butter side down in the pan. Top each slice of bread with a slice of Cheddar.

In a small skillet melt about a tablespoon of butter, and break the egg into the pan when it's hot. When the whites are cooked, break the yolk and spread it around a little and then flip it over. Quickly remove pan from heat.

As soon as the cheese melts and the buttered side of the bread is golden brown, place the egg and the bacon on top of the cheese on one of the slices of bread, and then top with the other slice, cheese side down, to form a sandwich.

Remove sandwich from skillet and cut in half so the golden yolk and melted cheese start to ooze out.

Devour at once!

# SWEDISH PANCAKES

*You can serve these so many ways. Fill with preserves, hazelnut spread, flavored cream cheese, sautéed apples, marmalade, or anything else your heart desires. Roll the filled pancakes or fold them in half and then in half again so you have triangles. Sprinkle with confectioners' sugar (just because it looks pretty) and drizzle with syrup or berry puree. They are just as delicious without any filling.*

**MAKES 4 SERVINGS.**

½ cup all-purpose flour

3 tablespoons sugar

⅛ teaspoon salt

4 large eggs

1 cup milk

⅓ cup melted butter, plus more for cooking

Whisk flour, sugar, and salt together in a small bowl. In a medium bowl whisk together eggs and milk. Whisk in the flour mixture, then the melted butter. Set aside for 5 minutes.

Place crepe pan or nonstick 8- or 9-inch skillet over medium heat. When pan is hot, brush with melted butter. Use a ladle to pour just enough batter to coat the bottom of the pan with a thin layer. (Depending on the size of pan, this will be around ⅓ to ½ cup.) Quickly swirl the pan to evenly coat the bottom with batter. Cook for about 1 minute or until bottom is golden brown. Gently loosen edges with a rubber spatula, and carefully flip. Cook an additional 30 seconds. Remove from pan and repeat process with the rest of the batter.

To keep pancakes warm, place them in a 200-degree oven.

**NOTE:** For a yummy glaze, stir ¼ cup orange marmalade into ¼ cup softened butter and heat to melt. Drizzle over crepes.

*Best-Ever Banana Bread (page 25)*

# BOUNTIFUL BREADS

SWEET AND SAVORY BAKED LOVE

All sorrows are less with bread.
—MIGUEL DE CERVANTES SAAVEDRA

**B**read comforts us in a way few other foods do. Pulling a rustic loaf of sourdough out of the oven as guests arrive makes them feel welcome. Delivering a cloth-lined basket filled with warm muffins to a lonely neighbor shows her you care. And sitting around the kitchen table, sharing a platter of cinnamon muffins with your kids, creates lifelong memories.

Bread has symbolized life and sharing for thousands of years. In the early church breaking bread was a part of fellowship. As we pass the bread basket around the dinner table, we share life together as the bread feeds our bodies and nourishes our souls.

## THE SWEET

Best-Ever Banana Bread

Apple Cider–Pumpkin Bread

Cranberry-Orange Muffins

Cinnamon Spice Donut Muffins

Mixed Berry Scones with Lemon Glaze

Cinnamon Scones

Raspberry Crumb Coffee Cake

Pumpkin Coffee Cake with Maple Glaze

## THE SAVORY

Tasty Bread

Southern Buttermilk Biscuits

Sweet Potato Biscuits

Cast-Iron Skillet Cornbread

Herbed Dinner Rolls

Cottage Herb Bread

Cheesy Onion Hedgehog Loaf

# BEST-EVER BANANA BREAD

*This recipe uses two to three overripe bananas. The bread freezes well so you can make a couple of loaves when you have the time and then pull one out of the freezer when your child tells you during breakfast that he promised you would bring a treat to class . . . today! (You know it's happened.)*

*This bread is extremely moist and flavorful and will quickly become the only banana bread you will ever make.*

**MAKES 1 LOAF.**

½ cup (1 stick) butter, softened, plus extra for preparing pan

1 ½ cups all-purpose flour

1 teaspoon salt

1 teaspoon baking soda

1 cup sugar

2 large eggs

½ cup sour cream

1 cup mashed bananas

1 teaspoon vanilla extract

½ cups chopped walnuts or pecans, optional

Preheat the oven to 350 degrees. Butter a 9 x 5-inch loaf pan.

In a small bowl sift together the flour, salt, and baking soda. In a large bowl cream together the softened butter and the sugar with a hand mixer or in a stand mixer. Add the eggs and blend well. Add the flour mixture and beat until smooth. Add the sour cream, bananas, and vanilla and beat until thoroughly blended. Stir in nuts, if using. Spoon batter into the loaf pan and bake for 1 hour or until toothpick comes out clean when inserted in the center.

Remove from the oven and cool on a wire rack for 10 minutes. Remove loaf from pan and continue to cool on cooling rack before slicing (if you can keep from eating it warm).

VARIATIONS: Add ⅔ cup mini semisweet chocolate chips or fresh blueberries (I omit the nuts when I use chips or blueberries).

# APPLE CIDER–PUMPKIN BREAD

*You can change this recipe up a little by using different add-ins. My favorite is mini chocolate chips. Pumpkin and chocolate go so well together! I also like it with pecans and then topped with a streusel topping. Well . . . I also like it with dried cranberries and pecans. You see my dilemma? Because the batter makes two loaves, sometimes I split it in half and make each with different add-ins so I don't have to choose.*

**MAKES 2 LOAVES.**

**BREAD**

3 cups all-purpose flour

1 tablespoon baking powder

2 teaspoons baking soda

2 teaspoons ground cinnamon

1 teaspoon ground nutmeg

¼ teaspoon ground cloves

3 cups sugar

1 cup vegetable oil

4 large eggs

1 (15-ounce) can pumpkin puree

⅔ cup apple cider (or use apple juice)

1 cup chopped pecans

1 cup raisins

**STREUSEL TOPPING**

⅓ cup all-purpose flour

2 tablespoons rolled oats

⅓ cup firmly packed light brown sugar

½ teaspoon ground cinnamon

¼ cup (½ stick) butter, cut into cubes, softened

½ cup chopped pecans

*To make the bread:*

Preheat the oven to 350 degrees. Grease and lightly flour two 9 x 5-inch loaf pans.

In a medium bowl whisk together flour, baking powder, baking soda, cinnamon, nutmeg, and cloves.

In a large bowl beat the sugar and oil until well combined with a hand mixer or in a stand mixer. Add the eggs, one at a time, beating after each addition. Add the flour mixture and beat until incorporated. Add a third of the pumpkin and beat until incorporated. Add a third of the apple cider and beat until incorporated. Repeat process adding a third of each until you have used all the pumpkin and cider. Stir in the pecans and raisins (or one of the variations below).

Divide the batter evenly between the two prepared loaf pans. (If your loaf pans are larger sizes, just fill them two-thirds full.)

*To make the topping:*

In a medium bowl combine the flour, oats, brown sugar, cinnamon, and butter with your fingers until the topping resembles coarse crumbs. Stir in the pecans. Sprinkle evenly over the batter.

Bake for 50 minutes or until a toothpick inserted in the center comes out clean. Remove from the oven and place on a cooling rack for 30 minutes. Remove from pans.

At this point you must force yourself not to eat an entire loaf while it is warm. Try . . . I don't think you can do it. But that's okay. There is a second loaf.

**VARIATIONS:** Add mini chocolate chips instead of the pecans and raisins.

Replace the raisins with dried cranberries.

# CRANBERRY-ORANGE MUFFINS

*Tart cranberries work so well with the sweetness of oranges. I add orange zest for a bit of brightness and sprinkle raw sugar over the tops before baking for a little crunch. The combination of flavors and textures is like a celebration in your mouth. Pile these colorful muffins in a towel-lined basket and deliver to a friend while they are still warm.*

**MAKES 12 MUFFINS.**

2 cups all-purpose flour
2 teaspoons baking powder
½ teaspoon baking soda
½ teaspoon salt
¼ teaspoon ground cinnamon
1 cup sugar, divided
1 cup fresh cranberries, chopped
¾ cup orange juice
¼ cup vegetable oil
½ cup sour cream
1 large egg, room temperature
1 teaspoon vanilla extract
Zest of 1 orange
3 tablespoons raw sugar

Preheat the oven to 400 degrees. Line 12 muffin cups with paper liners. Spray liners very lightly with nonstick cooking spray.

In a medium bowl whisk together flour, baking powder, baking soda, salt, and cinnamon. In a small bowl combine ¼ cup sugar with the chopped cranberries.

In a large bowl beat the remaining ¾ cup of the sugar with orange juice, oil, sour cream, egg, vanilla, and orange zest with a hand mixer or in a stand mixer. Add flour mixture and beat just until incorporated. Stir in cranberries.

Fill liners three-fourths full. Sprinkle with raw sugar. Bake for 16 to 18 minutes or until golden brown.

*I feel the happiest when I'm in my kitchen, preparing food for those I love. As I peel potatoes, chop herbs, and stir simmering pots of comfort, I pray God fills their lives with more love and more joy than their hearts could ever contain.*

# CINNAMON SPICE DONUT MUFFINS

*This recipe creates a delicious cross between a donut and a muffin. If there is someone in your life who could use some encouragement, a shoulder to cry on, or just someone who will listen, invite him or her to share these gems along with a hot cup of coffee. Warm muffins and a friend who genuinely cares will comfort a hurting heart.*

**MAKES 12 STANDARD OR 30 MINI MUFFINS.**

**MUFFINS**

3 cups all-purpose flour
1 tablespoon baking powder
½ teaspoon baking soda
1 teaspoon salt
1 teaspoon ground cinnamon
½ teaspoon ground nutmeg
¼ teaspoon pumpkin pie spice
1 cup (2 sticks) butter, softened
1 cup sugar
2 large eggs, room temperature
1 cup milk
1 teaspoon vanilla extract

**CINNAMON SUGAR TOPPING**

½ cup (1 stick) butter
1 cup sugar
2 teaspoons ground cinnamon

*To make the muffins:*

Preheat the oven to 350 degrees. Line muffin tins with liners.

In a medium bowl whisk together the flour, baking powder, baking soda, salt, cinnamon, nutmeg, and pumpkin pie spice.

In a large bowl cream the butter and sugar together with a hand mixer or in a stand mixer until fluffy. Add the eggs, one at a time, beating after each one until just incorporated. Pour the milk into a small bowl. Add the vanilla and stir to combine. Beat a third of the vanilla milk into the butter mixture until incorporated, then a third of the flour mixture until incorporated. Repeat in thirds until everything is combined. Do not overmix.

Fill the muffin liners three-fourths full. Bake standard-size muffins for 25 minutes or mini muffins for 18 minutes. Test doneness by inserting a toothpick into the center of a muffin. The muffins are done when the toothpick comes out clean.

*To make the topping:*

Melt butter in bowl just wide enough to fit muffins. In a small bowl combine the sugar and cinnamon. As soon as the muffins are cool enough to handle, dip the tops into the melted butter. Then dip into the cinnamon sugar mixture. Serve warm.

# MIXED BERRY SCONES WITH LEMON GLAZE

*Scones are my favorite coffee shop treat. They are a little denser and drier than biscuits, making them perfect for enjoying with a mug of your favorite hot beverage. The combination of berries and lemon makes this version refreshingly bright. They are as beautiful as they are delicious. A warm batch is a wonderful way to love on someone. Arrange them in a basket lined with a pretty, colorful towel, and give them as a gift. Write a favorite verse on a pretty note card and tuck it inside. It truly will be a basket full of love!*

**MAKES 18 SCONES.**

3 ¼ cups all-purpose flour

⅓ cup sugar

1 tablespoon baking powder

½ teaspoon baking soda

¾ teaspoon ground cinnamon

1 teaspoon salt

Zest of 1 lemon

6 tablespoons butter, frozen

2 cups mixed berries (raspberries, blackberries, blueberries)

1 ⅓ cups buttermilk

Raw sugar

Lemon Glaze (next page)

In a large bowl combine the flour, sugar, baking powder, baking soda, cinnamon, salt, and lemon zest. Whisk together until combined. Grate the frozen butter on a box grater and stir into flour mixture with a whisk. Stir in the berries.

Add the buttermilk and gently stir just until combined. When barely combined, gently knead together with your hands in the bowl (some of the berries will break down but some will remain whole). The dough will be very sticky. Do not overwork the dough or your scones will be tough.

When completely combined, drop tangerine-size blobs on ungreased, jelly-roll pan 2 inches apart. Set the cookie sheet in the refrigerator for 1 hour (or cover and leave overnight).

Preheat the oven to 425 degrees. Sprinkle the scones with raw sugar. Bake for 15–20 minutes or until golden. Remove from the oven and let rest on the cookie sheets for 5–10 minutes. Spoon the Lemon Glaze on the warm scones and serve warm.

### LEMON GLAZE

Zest and the juice of 1 lemon

1 ½ cups confectioners' sugar, sifted

1 tablespoon butter, melted

In a small bowl combine the lemon zest and juice, confectioners' sugar, and butter with a whisk until smooth. (This is best made the day before. Store covered in the refrigerator and then take it out to soften while the scones are baking. Don't worry if it's thick. The glaze will melt over the warm scones when you spoon it on.)

*Dear Lord, don't let me miss out on the good works You would have me do today. Open my eyes to the hurting hearts around me. Amen.*

# CINNAMON SCONES

*The secret to making perfect scones is in the butter. After much experimenting I have discovered grating the butter instead of cutting it into small cubes results in a more even distribution of butter and creates a more tender scone. This recipe will fill your home with the most amazing aroma. Enjoy them as soon as they come out of the oven for a warm, cinnamony fall morning treat.*

**MAKES 16 SCONES.**

3 ¼ cups all-purpose flour

⅓ cup plus 1 tablespoon sugar, divided

1 tablespoon baking powder

½ teaspoon baking soda

2 teaspoons ground cinnamon, divided

1 teaspoon salt

6 tablespoons butter, frozen

1 ½ cups cinnamon chips

1 ⅓ cups buttermilk

3 tablespoons butter, melted

In a large bowl combine the flour, ⅓ cup sugar, baking powder, baking soda, 1 teaspoon cinnamon, and salt. Grate the butter using a box grater, and mix into the flour mixture with your fingers. Stir in the cinnamon chips. Add the buttermilk and stir until combined. (Do not overmix or your scones will be tough.)

Turn the dough out onto a lightly floured surface. Gently knead just until the dough comes together. Divide the dough in half and pat each out into a ½-inch-thick disk. Brush with the melted butter. In a small bowl combine the remaining 1 tablespoon sugar with 1 teaspoon cinnamon and sprinkle over the butter-coated dough.

Cut each disk into 8 wedges (like pizza slices). Arrange the wedges 2 inches apart on two cookie sheets lined with parchment paper. Place in the refrigerator for 45 minutes. (Do not skip this step. If you don't allow the dough to chill, the scones will spread on your cookie sheets.)

Preheat the oven to 425 degrees. Bake the scones for 14 minutes. (You will probably need to cook in two batches—one at a time.) Remove from the oven and let sit on cookie sheets for 5 to 10 minutes before serving.

NOTE: You can find cinnamon chips near the chocolate chips in your grocery store. If your store doesn't carry them, there are several online sources.

# RASPBERRY CRUMB COFFEE CAKE

*Everyone knows the best part of a crumb cake is the crumb topping. The more crumbs, the better, so I've really piled them on. You can use any berry or combination of berries in this coffee cake. It's important to make the crumb topping before making the cake batter. The melted butter will firm up as it sits so you can crumble it after the batter is in the pan.*

**MAKES 10 SERVINGS.**

**CRUMB TOPPING**

¾ cup light brown sugar

½ cup sugar

1 teaspoon ground cinnamon

⅛ teaspoon ground nutmeg

¼ teaspoon salt

6 tablespoons butter, melted

1 ⅔ cups all-purpose flour

**CAKE**

1 ½ cups cake flour

1 teaspoon baking powder

½ teaspoon baking soda

½ teaspoon salt

½ cup (1 stick) butter, softened

½ cup sugar

¼ cup firmly packed light brown sugar

1 large egg

⅔ cup sour cream

1 teaspoon vanilla extract

1 ½ cups raspberries

Confectioners' sugar

*To make the crumb topping:*

Preheat the oven to 350 degrees. Butter and lightly flour an 8-inch springform pan.

In a medium bowl combine brown sugar, sugar, cinnamon, nutmeg, and salt. Mix in the melted butter. Once combined, stir in the flour.

*To make the cake:*

In a medium bowl whisk together the cake flour, baking powder, baking soda, and salt. In a large bowl beat the butter, sugar, and brown sugar for 3 minutes with a hand mixer or in a stand mixer. Add the egg, sour cream, and vanilla and beat until combined. Add the flour mixture and beat just until incorporated.

Spread the batter into the springform pan with a spatula. Arrange the raspberries over the batter. Use your hands to crumble the topping and distribute evenly over the raspberries.

Bake for 50 minutes or until the crumbs are golden. Remove from the oven and place on a rack to cool.

After 30 minutes, loosen and remove the ring from the springform pan. Cool completely. Use a spatula to carefully remove the cake from the bottom of the pan and slide onto a serving dish. Generously dust with confectioners' sugar.

NOTE: If you don't have a springform pan, you can use a deep round cake layer pan or an 8 x 8-inch square baking pan. If not baking in a springform pan, do not remove the coffee cake from the pan before serving.

**VARIATION:** This coffee cake is also yummy with sliced peaches. Just replace half of the vanilla extract with almond extract.

*If you want to feel the richness and warmth of unfailing love, give it. If you want to make a difference and leave your world a better place, let others know how important they are as you put their needs above yours.*

**—JAREN L. DAVIS**

# PUMPKIN COFFEE CAKE WITH MAPLE GLAZE

*There are no words to describe this goodness. You need to make this as quickly as possible. Your house will smell indescribably delicious and your family will bow before you with gratitude and offers to do the dishes.*

**MAKES 16 SERVINGS.**

### CAKE

1 (15-ounce) can pumpkin puree
⅓ cup apple juice
2 large eggs
2 tablespoons vegetable oil
2 teaspoons vanilla extract
2 teaspoons pumpkin pie spice
1 (18.25-ounce) box yellow cake mix

### STREUSEL

6 tablespoons butter, melted
¾ cup brown sugar
¾ cup all-purpose flour
1 teaspoon ground cinnamon
¾ cup chopped pecans

### GLAZE

½ cup brown sugar
¼ cup heavy cream
¼ cup pure maple syrup

*To make the cake:*

Preheat the oven to 350 degrees. Spray a 9 x 13-inch baking pan with nonstick cooking spray.

In a large bowl combine the pumpkin puree, apple juice, eggs, oil, vanilla, and pumpkin pie spice with a wire whisk. Stir in the cake mix and pour into the pan.

*To make the streusel:*

In a small bowl combine the butter, brown sugar, flour, and cinnamon. Once combined, mix in the pecans. Crumble with your fingers and evenly distribute over the cake.

Bake for 30 to 40 minutes or until a toothpick inserted in the center comes out clean.

*To make the glaze:*

After the cake comes out of the oven, combine the brown sugar, cream, and maple syrup in a small saucepan and bring to a simmer over medium-low heat, stirring frequently. Simmer until the sugar has dissolved and the glaze is thick (3 to 5 minutes).

With a large carving fork or skewer, poke holes all over the top of the warm cake. Pour the warm glaze evenly over the cake and set aside for 30 minutes before serving.

# TASTY BREAD

*These buttery morsels of goodness were named by my favorite little girl, Jackie. Jackie was about three years old at the time and was a very picky eater. VERY PICKY! She took one bite of these biscuits and declared them "tasty bread!" From that moment on, every time Jackie brought her mommy, daddy, and baby brother to my house for dinner, she asked if we were having Tasty Bread. If a picky three-year-old likes these biscuits, you know you have a winner!*

**MAKES 12 BISCUITS.**

**BISCUITS**

1 ¾ cups all-purpose flour

1 tablespoon plus 2 teaspoons baking powder

1 tablespoon sugar

½ teaspoon salt

3 tablespoons vegetable shortening, softened

4 tablespoons cold butter, cubed

1 ⅓ cups shredded sharp Cheddar cheese

¾ cup milk

**GARLIC BUTTER**

6 tablespoons butter, melted

2 cloves garlic, minced

1 tablespoon chopped fresh parsley

*To make the biscuits:*

Preheat the oven to 425 degrees. Lightly spray a cookie sheet with nonstick cooking spray.

Combine the flour, baking powder, sugar, and salt in a large bowl. Add the shortening and butter and blend with a pastry cutter until well combined. Stir in the Cheddar cheese. Pour in the milk and stir until the mixture is moistened.

Flour your hands and gently knead the dough in the bowl just until it forms a ball. Do not overwork the dough or the biscuits will be tough. Drop the dough onto the prepared cookie sheet in ¼ cup portions, 2 inches apart. Bake for 15 to 20 minutes or until golden.

*To make the garlic butter:*

Combine the butter, garlic, and parsley in a small bowl. When the biscuits come out of the oven, brush with the garlic butter.

Go ahead . . . try to eat just one.

# SOUTHERN BUTTERMILK BISCUITS

*Every good Southern gal has a favorite biscuit recipe. This is mine. Biscuits are the best comfort food. They are great with breakfast or dinner (or supper, as we say in the South). Serve them warm with butter and jam or with gravy. Cut leftovers in half, toast, and use to make a sandwich with a fried chicken strip and a generous drizzle of honey.*

**MAKES 8 BISCUITS.**

1 ½ cups all-purpose flour

¾ cup cake flour

3 teaspoons baking powder

½ teaspoon baking soda

¾ teaspoon salt

½ cup (1 stick) butter, cut into small pieces (keep in refrigerator until ready to use)

2 tablespoons shortening (keep in refrigerator until ready to use)

1 cup buttermilk, cold

Line a cookie sheet with parchment paper.

In a large bowl whisk together the all-purpose flour and cake flour, baking powder, baking soda, and salt. Add the butter and shortening and cut into the flour mixture with a pastry blender or your fingers until the dough resembles coarse crumbs. Quickly stir in the buttermilk, only until combined.

Turn the dough out onto a lightly floured surface and knead the dough, adding flour as necessary to keep it from sticking to the surface and your hands. Only knead the dough until it comes together. Do not overmix or the biscuits will be tough.

Roll or flatten the dough with your hands, pressing the dough into a slab about ¾ inch thick. Cut the biscuits with a biscuit cutter or into squares with a knife. Place on the cookie sheet and cover with plastic wrap or a towel and set aside for 30 minutes to rest.

While the biscuits are resting, preheat oven to 425 degrees. Bake biscuits for 12 to 15 minutes or until golden brown. Serve warm. My favorite way to enjoy them is with a pat of softened butter and homemade strawberry jam. My eyes are tearing up just thinking about them.

# SWEET POTATO BISCUITS

*These are a delightful version of biscuits often gracing Southern tables during the holidays. I love to serve them with honey butter. If you have any left over, warm them, split them in half, spread with honey nut cream cheese, and add a slice of honey-roasted ham.*

**MAKES 16 TO 18 BISCUITS.**

1 ¾ cups all-purpose flour

2 ½ teaspoons baking powder

1 teaspoon baking soda

1 teaspoon salt

3 tablespoons light brown sugar, plus more for tops

⅛ teaspoon ground cinnamon

6 tablespoons butter, cold and cut into tiny cubes

1 cup pureed sweet potatoes, cold

⅓ cup plus 2 tablespoons cold buttermilk

2 tablespoons butter, melted (for tops)

Honey butter for serving (see note)

Preheat the oven to 425 degrees. Lightly spray a cookie sheet with nonstick cooking spray or line with parchment paper.

In a large bowl combine flour, baking powder, baking soda, salt, brown sugar, and cinnamon. Whisk until smooth. Add butter pieces to the flour mixture and use a pastry blender or your fingers to cut the butter into the flour until the mixture resembles coarse crumbs.

In a small bowl combine sweet potatoes and buttermilk. Stir until smooth, then stir into the flour mixture. Stir only until the mixture comes together. If the mixture is too dry and won't come together, add a little more buttermilk.

Gather up the dough and turn it out onto a lightly floured surface. Use your hands to gently press out the dough so it is 1 inch thick. Use a 2-inch cookie or biscuit cutter to cut the dough. Do not twist the cutter when cutting biscuits so they will rise evenly. Place on the prepared cookie sheet. Brush the tops with melted butter and sprinkle with brown sugar (about 1 teaspoon per biscuit).

Bake for 20 to 25 minutes or until golden brown. Let sit on the cookie sheet for 5 minutes. Then remove and serve warm with honey butter.

NOTE: You can find honey butter next to the butter in your grocery store, or you can make your own. Simply cream ¼ cup honey into 6 tablespoons softened butter until smooth.

# CAST-IRON SKILLET CORNBREAD

*I don't think I could live without my cast-iron skillet. One pan should last a lifetime—actually, it should last a few lifetimes. Cast-iron pans are passed down from generation to generation, each adding a layer of seasoning and love and stories to the pan. It's a family treasure. Mine wasn't passed down, but I sure hope the love I'm putting into it now will be enjoyed by future generations.*

**MAKES 8 SERVINGS.**

1 ½ cups cornmeal

⅔ cup all-purpose flour

3 tablespoons sugar

2 teaspoons baking powder

½ teaspoon baking soda

1 teaspoon salt

1 cup plus 3 tablespoons buttermilk

⅓ cup sour cream

2 large eggs, lightly beaten

5 tablespoons butter, divided

Set a 9- or 10-inch cast-iron skillet on the center rack in the oven and preheat the oven to 425 degrees.

In a medium bowl whisk together cornmeal, flour, sugar, baking powder, baking soda, and salt. In another medium bowl whisk together buttermilk, sour cream, and eggs. Stir the buttermilk mixture into the cornmeal mixture. Melt 4 tablespoons of the butter and stir into the batter just until combined.

Remove the hot skillet from the oven and place the last tablespoon of butter into the pan, moving it around to melt and coat the skillet.

Transfer the batter into the hot, buttered skillet and return to the oven. Bake for 18 to 22 minutes or until golden brown and starting to pull away from the sides of the skillet. Remove from the oven and serve hot right from the skillet (with plenty of butter or honey butter, of course).

# HERBED DINNER ROLLS

*This is an easy shortcut method for making "homemade" dinner rolls. Change the herbs to complement your entrée. I like to use various combinations of chives, parsley, rosemary, and thyme. I find this recipe works best if you keep it simple, using just one or two herbs at a time.*

**MAKES 8 ROLLS.**

⅓ cup butter, plus extra for preparing dish

8 frozen, un-risen dinner rolls

2 tablespoons finely chopped fresh herbs

1 teaspoon coarse sea salt

Butter a baking dish large enough to hold rolls with about 1 inch in between each roll to give them room to rise. (They will probably double in size.) Remove the rolls from the package and arrange in the buttered dish. Cover the rolls with a towel or plastic wrap and place in a warm, draft-free place to rise for 2 hours.

Melt the butter and brush the risen rolls liberally. Sprinkle evenly with the chopped herbs and salt. Bake as directed on package. Serve warm.

> *The way I see it, my kitchen is a sanctuary of nourishment and discovery, full of warm smells, flavors, and experiences that will hopefully bake into a memory that will last my children a lifetime.*
>
> **—TYLER FLORENCE**

# COTTAGE HERB BREAD

*I try to have something ready to come out of the oven when I'm expecting guests, and nothing says "welcome" like the aroma of homemade herb bread. If you have any leftovers, which is unlikely, toast a slice and spread butter over the warm, toasty bread so it melts into the nooks and crannies. Also great to serve with a bowl of soup!*

**MAKES 1 LOAF.**

1 (.25 ounce) envelope active dry yeast

⅓ cup warm, not hot, water

1 teaspoon sugar

3 tablespoons butter, divided, plus extra to coat bowl

1 cup small-curd cottage cheese

1 teaspoon salt

2 tablespoons dry minced onions

2 teaspoons dill seed

2 tablespoons chopped chives

3 tablespoons honey

1 large egg, room temperature

2 ⅓ cups all-purpose flour

½ teaspoon baking soda

In a small bowl combine yeast, warm water, and sugar and set aside for 10 minutes to allow the yeast to proof. You will know the yeast has proofed when you see a creamy foam on the surface of the water (see note).

Place 2 tablespoons butter in a saucepan over medium-low heat. As soon as the butter has melted, stir in the cottage cheese, salt, minced onions, dill seed, chives, and honey. Continue to cook and stir until warm, but not hot. Remove from the heat and quickly whisk in the egg.

In a large bowl combine the flour and baking soda with a whisk. Add the yeast mixture to the cottage cheese mixture and stir to combine. Pour into the flour mixture and stir until completely combined.

Butter a large bowl and transfer the dough to the bowl. Cover with a towel and place in a warm spot for 1 hour to rise. The dough should double in size. Punch down the dough. Butter a 9-inch loaf pan and turn batter into pan. Cover with a towel and let rise another hour or until doubled in size.

Preheat the oven to 350 degrees. Melt the remaining 1 tablespoon butter in a small bowl. Remove the towel from the dough and brush the top with butter. Bake for 35 to 40 minutes or until a toothpick inserted in the center comes out clean and the top is a deep golden brown.

Let sit in the pan for 10 minutes, and then remove, slice, and serve warm with butter.

NOTE: It's a good idea to have extra packets of yeast. If the first doesn't proof, you will have a backup. And always check the expiration date on the packages.

# CHEESY ONION HEDGEHOG LOAF

*This bread is just plain fun! It looks spectacular when you bring it to the table, and it's a great bread to share. Just place it in the center of the table and let everyone grab cheesy pieces family-style. It encourages conversation and laughter. It's "bonding bread"!*

**MAKES 4 TO 6 SERVINGS.**

1 large rustic sourdough boule

8 ounces Cheddar, mozzarella, Swiss, or Pepper Jack cheese, thinly sliced

½ cup (1 stick) butter, melted

2 green onions, finely chopped

2 cloves garlic, minced

Preheat the oven to 350 degrees.

Without cutting all the way through to the bottom of the bread, use a sharp bread knife to make deep cuts from top to bottom at 1 ½-inch intervals. Turn the loaf and slice in the other direction to create tall squares of bread. Tuck slices of cheese into the cuts in the bread.

In a small bowl combine the melted butter, green onions, and garlic, and drizzle into the slits and over the entire loaf. Wrap the bread in foil and place on a cookie sheet. Bake for 15 minutes. Unwrap and continue baking for 10 to 15 minutes or until the cheese has melted and the bread is crispy.

# STARTERS AND SALADS

## DIPS, TINY MORSELS, AND FRESH SALADS

No eye has seen, no ear has heard, and no mind has imagined
what God has prepared for those who love him.
—1 CORINTHIANS 2:9 NLT

That very first bite sets the tone for the rest of the meal. It's like a preview of what is to come, just as a beautifully wrapped package hints at the special contents within. The anticipation of what awaits is part of the experience. Those first bites should be savored the same way a gift should be slowly unwrapped, not ripped apart.

Similarly, a spectacular sunset, the fragrance of a field of wildflowers, the sound of birds singing, and the fruits of the Spirit seen through the words and actions of others are mere glimpses of God's glory.

Slow down and enjoy the sunset. Take time to smell the field of wildflowers and listen to the musical conversations of the birds. And let others see His glory in you by extending kindness, gentleness, and goodness to those around you. We can never imagine the feast God is preparing for us, but let's savor the foretaste of the glory that awaits those who love Him.

## STARTERS

Baked Crab Dip

Ooey Gooey Mexi Dip

Endive Salad Spears

Italian Stuffed Mushrooms

Hot Sausage and Spinach Dip

Blue Cheese Dip

Caprese Poppers

Caramelized Onion and Bacon Crostini

Sweet and Savory Chicken Bites

## SALADS

Autumn Salad with Pecan-Crusted Bacon

Colorful Waldorf Salad

New Potato Salad

Coleslaw

Wild Rice Salad

Primavera Pasta Salad

Upside-Down Chicken Paillard Salad

Grilled Chicken and Berry Salad

Pico De Gallo Salad

# STARTERS

There's a lot of power in a platter filled with a variety of tasty morsels of goodness. Placing a dish to be shared in the middle of a coffee table encourages mingling between friends and conversations between strangers. Well . . . former strangers. The more delicious and tempting the dish, the more power it holds. These recipes are guaranteed to bring people together.

## BAKED CRAB DIP

*If you want to make friends really fast, serve this warm, cheesy crab dip. They will love you and invite you to all their parties. Of course, they will ask you to bring your amazing crab dip.*

**MAKES 8 SERVINGS.**

⅔ cup sour cream

⅔ cup mayonnaise

3 green onions, chopped

2 cloves garlic, minced

2 teaspoons chopped chives

1 ½ cups grated Parmesan cheese, divided

1 cup shredded Swiss cheese

1 cup shredded Cheddar cheese

2 tablespoons freshly squeezed lemon juice

2 tablespoons Worcestershire sauce

4 tablespoons chopped fresh parsley, divided

¼ teaspoon cayenne pepper (or to taste)

¼ teaspoon salt

¼ teaspoon black pepper

1 pound jumbo lump crabmeat

Preheat the oven to 325 degrees. Spray a shallow casserole dish or pie dish with nonstick cooking spray.

In a large bowl combine sour cream, mayonnaise, green onions, garlic, chives, 1 cup Parmesan cheese, Swiss cheese, Cheddar cheese, lemon juice, Worcestershire, 2 tablespoons parsley, cayenne pepper, salt, and black pepper. When thoroughly combined, stir in the crabmeat. Spoon the mixture into the prepared dish. Sprinkle with the remaining ½ cup Parmesan cheese.

Bake for 40 minutes or until bubbly and golden. Remove from the oven and sprinkle with the remaining 2 tablespoons parsley. Serve hot with crackers or toasted bread rounds.

# OOEY GOOEY MEXI DIP

*I'm not much of a sport fan unless my kid is playing. But while I don't love sports, I do love cooking for sports fans, and Ooey Gooey Mexi Dip is a fan favorite! Serve this hot with a pile of tortilla chips, and I promise that all sporting events will be watched from your house from then on. Now, if you don't want a house full of screaming fans, don't make Ooey Gooey Mexi Dip, because there will be no way to keep them out!*

**SERVES 8 FANS OR 2 OFFENSIVE LINEMEN.**

1 (16-ounce) can traditional refried beans

3 cups shredded Mexican cheese blend, divided

¼ cup mayonnaise

¾ cup sour cream

1 (4.25-ounce) can sliced olives, drained (set aside 1 tablespoon)

1 (4-ounce) can chopped green chilies, drained

2 cloves garlic, minced

3 green onions, sliced (set aside 1 tablespoon)

1 medium tomato, chopped

Preheat the oven to 350 degrees.

Spray a quiche or pie dish with nonstick cooking spray. Spread the refried beans evenly in the bottom of the pan.

In a medium bowl combine 2 cups of the cheese, mayonnaise, sour cream, olives, chilies, garlic, and green onions. (Leave out the reserved olives and green onions.) Spread the mixture over the layer of beans and top with the remaining 1 cup of cheese. Sprinkle with the reserved olives and green onions.

Bake for 25 to 30 minutes or until hot and bubbly. Remove from the oven and top with chopped tomatoes. Serve with tortilla chips.

# ENDIVE SALAD SPEARS

*These little treasures are delicious as well as beautiful. You could serve them on a platter as an appetizer or you could arrange a few of them on an individual salad dish for each person. I like to arrange them decoratively on a large platter and set it on my coffee table for friends to share before dinner. Serving them this way creates a relaxed atmosphere, setting the perfect tone for conversation.*

**MAKES 6 TO 8 SERVINGS AS APPETIZERS.**

½ cup balsamic vinegar

6 tablespoons orange juice

2 tablespoon honey

Dash or two of cayenne pepper

16 endive leaves (3 to 4 heads)

2 pears, finely chopped

½ cup blue cheese crumbles

½ cup dried cranberries

½ cup chopped pecan pie–glazed pecans (find them near mixed nuts and snacks)

Combine balsamic vinegar, orange juice, honey, and cayenne pepper in a small saucepan and simmer over low heat until reduced by half. Remove from heat and cool completely.

Separate the endive leaves by cutting about ½ an inch off the root end holding the leaves together. Rinse leaves and lay on paper towels to dry. In a medium bowl combine the pears, blue cheese, dried cranberries, and pecans. Spoon a tablespoon of the filling on the tip of each spear.

Arrange filled spears on serving platter or on individual salad plates. Drizzle with balsamic vinegar mixture.

# ITALIAN STUFFED MUSHROOMS

*This is the only appetizer the Italian side of my family ever made. The aroma of garlic and cheese brings back memories of a house filled with loud Italians laughing, yelling, cooking, eating, and loving. I only have three recipes from this side of my family, and I treasure each one because they keep these memories alive and keep me connected to the generations before mine.*

**MAKES 8 SERVINGS.**

2 cloves garlic, minced

½ cup (1 stick) butter, melted

1 cup Italian-style bread crumbs

¾ cup grated Parmesan cheese, divided

¼ cup chopped fresh parsley

1 ½ to 2 pounds fresh mushrooms, stemmed and wiped clean

Olive oil

½ cup shredded mozzarella cheese

Preheat the oven to 375 degrees.

In a medium bowl mix the garlic into the melted butter. Stir in bread crumbs, ½ cup of the Parmesan cheese, and the parsley.

Arrange the mushroom caps on a jelly-roll pan and drizzle very lightly with olive oil. Fill each mushroom cap three-fourths full with the bread crumb mixture. Divide all of the mozzarella cheese among the mushrooms. Top the mozzarella with the remaining bread crumb mixture so the crumbs are mounded above the top of the mushroom cap. Sprinkle with the remaining ¼ cup of Parmesan cheese and drizzle very lightly with additional olive oil.

Bake for 25 to 30 minutes or until the cheese has melted and the tops are golden brown. Serve hot.

# HOT SAUSAGE AND SPINACH DIP

*This hearty dip is perfect for a group gathering to watch a big game. I used to refer to it as my "Manly Man" dip until three girlfriends sat down and ate the entire thing in one sitting!*

**MAKES 8 TO 12 SERVINGS.**

1 pound ground sausage, mild or spicy or combination of both

2 tablespoons butter

1 onion, finely chopped

1 red bell pepper, chopped

3 cloves garlic, minced

1 (16-ounce) can cannellini or navy, rinsed and drained

½ cup chicken stock

⅓ cup chopped fresh parsley

2 (8-ounce) packages cream cheese cut into cubes, softened

½ cup sour cream

1 (5-ounce) package baby spinach leaves

1 cup grated Parmesan cheese

2 cups shredded Monterey Jack cheese

Preheat the oven to 350 degrees. Spray a shallow 2-quart casserole dish with nonstick cooking spray.

Brown the sausage in a heavy skillet over medium heat. Drain the grease, and then add the butter, onions, and red peppers to the skillet. Continue to cook, stirring occasionally, for 5 minutes. Stir in the garlic, beans, chicken stock, and parsley and simmer for 1 minute. Add the cream cheese and sour cream, cooking and stirring until the cream cheese has melted. Stir in the spinach until wilted. Add the Parmesan cheese and stir to combine. Spoon the mixture into the casserole dish. Top with the Monterey Jack cheese. Bake for 20 to 25 minutes or until the cheese has melted and the mixture is hot and bubbly.

# BLUE CHEESE DIP

*This dip is a hit with blue cheese lovers and those, like me, who are not lovers of the blue stuff. I think it's because the blue cheese flavor is there but there are no big chunks to bite into. I like to serve this with assorted raw veggies for dipping, but it's also good with thick-cut chips (delicate chips will break in this thick and rich dip) or even buffalo wings.*

**MAKES 2 CUPS.**

4 ounces cream cheese, softened

1 cup sour cream

¼ cup mayonnaise

1 teaspoon Worcestershire sauce

4 ounces blue cheese crumbles

½ teaspoon black pepper

1 tablespoon chopped fresh chives, plus more for garnish

In a medium bowl use a hand mixer or a stand mixer to beat the cream cheese until it is smooth and creamy. Add the sour cream, mayonnaise, and Worcestershire and continue beating until well combined. Set aside a little of the blue cheese to use as a garnish and add the rest to the creamy mixture. Beat until the blue cheese has been blended into the cream cheese mixture and only very small bits of cheese can be seen. Add the pepper and the chives and beat only until blended.

Cover and store in the refrigerator for at least 2 hours so the flavors can meld. When ready to serve, transfer the dip to a serving dish and top with the reserved blue cheese crumbles and chives for color, if desired.

# CAPRESE POPPERS

*When tomatoes are in season, tomato, mozzarella, and basil with homemade vinaigrette is one of my favorite salads. When I needed a colorful appetizer for an event I was catering several years ago, I decided to create a bite-size version of the salad using cherry tomatoes. They were the favorite item on the menu, and I've been making them ever since.*

**MAKES 8 TO 10 SERVINGS.**

4 tablespoons extra-virgin olive oil

2 tablespoons cider vinegar

2 tablespoons balsamic vinegar

1 tablespoon minced shallot

1 clove garlic, minced

2 teaspoons grated Parmesan cheese

Salt and black pepper to taste

1 package cherry tomatoes

1 ball mozzarella cheese, cut into thin 1-inch strips

5 to 6 basil leaves, torn into small pieces, plus more for garnish

In a small bowl combine the oil, cider and balsamic vinegars, shallot, garlic, Parmesan cheese, and salt and pepper.

Slice off the very top of each tomato and then carefully remove the juice and seeds using a small spoon. Fill each tomato with ½ teaspoon of the dressing. Then place a piece of mozzarella and a piece of basil in each, so the cheese and basil rise above the top of the tomato. Arrange on a platter and garnish with a fresh bunch of basil.

# CARAMELIZED ONION AND BACON CROSTINI

*This appetizer takes a little effort, but it is sooooo worth it. It rings all the bells! They are sweet, savory, crunchy, and cheesy. You know . . . your four basic food groups!*

**MAKES 8 TO 10 SERVINGS.**

2 ½ feet of French baguettes, cut into ½-inch slices

4 tablespoons butter, divided

5 slices bacon, cut into ½-inch strips

2 large onions, peeled, cut into four wedges, and then thinly sliced

¾ teaspoon salt, divided

1 tablespoon brown sugar

1 tablespoon cider vinegar

3 ounces cream cheese, softened

⅓ cup sour cream

⅓ cup mayonnaise

½ teaspoon dried thyme

¼ teaspoon black pepper

¼ teaspoon garlic powder

½ cup shredded Swiss cheese

½ cup shredded Cheddar cheese

Preheat oven to 400 degrees. Place the baguette slices on a cookie sheet. Melt 3 tablespoons of the butter and brush onto the baguette slices. Bake for 8 minutes and remove from the oven. Reduce the oven temperature to 375 degrees.

In a large skillet over medium heat, brown the bacon. Remove the bits with a slotted spoon and drain on paper towels.

Add the remaining tablespoon of butter to the pan with the bacon grease. As soon as the butter has melted, increase the temperature to medium-high and add the onions. Cook and stir for 2 minutes. Add ½ teaspoon salt and the brown sugar. Cook, stirring often, for 10 minutes. Reduce the heat to medium and continue to cook, stirring often, for 20 to 30 minutes or until the onions are deep golden brown.

Add the vinegar, stirring to scrape up bits from the bottom of the skillet. Remove from the heat.

In a medium bowl combine the cream cheese, sour cream, and mayonnaise. Stir in the thyme, the remaining ¼ teaspoon salt, pepper, and garlic powder. Add the Swiss and Cheddar cheeses and stir to combine. Stir in the onions and bacon bits.

Spread about 3 tablespoons of the mixture onto the toasted baguette slices and return to the cookie sheet. Bake for 8 to 10 minutes or until hot and the cheese has melted.

# SWEET AND SAVORY CHICKEN BITES

*This is one of my favorite appetizers. They are extremely messy to make but well worth the sticky fingers and countertop. They always disappear as quickly as I can pull a batch out of the oven. At one event I actually caught a man piling them on his plate and then hiding the plate so no one would find them.*

*Don't let the amount of cayenne scare you. It isn't at all overwhelming and the cayenne balances the sweetness.*

**MAKES 50 TO 60 PIECES.**

1 cup soy sauce

½ cup vegetable oil

½ cup sugar

½ cup honey

5 cloves garlic, minced

½ teaspoon five-spice powder

¼ teaspoon ground white pepper

½ cup toasted sesame seeds

6 boneless, skinless chicken breasts, cut into 1-inch cubes

1 ½ cups brown sugar

1 (1-ounce) container chili powder

2 to 3 teaspoons cayenne pepper (according to taste)

2 pounds bacon, each slice cut into thirds

In a medium bowl combine the soy sauce, oil, sugar, honey, garlic, five-spice powder, white pepper, and sesame seeds. Place cubed chicken in a shallow dish or a sealable plastic bag. Pour the soy mixture over the chicken. Cover dish or seal the bag and refrigerate for several hours or overnight.

When ready to assemble, combine the brown sugar, chili powder, and cayenne in a shallow dish.

Preheat the oven to 425 degrees. Line a jelly-roll pan with foil.

Remove the chicken from the marinade and discard the marinade. Wrap a piece of the bacon around each chicken cube and secure with a toothpick. Coat evenly with the brown sugar mixture and place on the prepared cookie sheet. Bake for 20 minutes or until the bacon is crispy and brown. Serve immediately. (Do you hear that? Listen. It's the hallelujah choir!)

# SALADS

As an accompaniment to a meal, the flavors of a salad should complement the entrée. As a main course, a salad should be a work of art. Salads are a great way to feature fresh ingredients and combinations of flavors and textures. You are only limited by your own imagination.

*Autumn Salad with Pecan-Crusted Bacon (page 62)*

# AUTUMN SALAD WITH PECAN-CRUSTED BACON

*You're going to read this recipe and think there is way too much bacon, but trust me, if you don't make extra you won't have any for the salads because people will eat this sweet and salty treat like it's candy.*

**MAKES 4 SERVINGS.**

**PECAN CRUSTED BACON**

2 cups finely chopped pecans
½ cup light brown sugar
½ cup pure maple syrup
1 pound thick-sliced bacon

**DRESSING**

6 tablespoons extra-virgin olive oil
3 tablespoons cider vinegar
3 tablespoons balsamic vinegar
1 heaping tablespoon Dijon mustard
2 tablespoons pure maple syrup
1 small shallot, minced
½ teaspoon salt
½ teaspoon black pepper

**SALAD**

6 cups baby lettuce leaves
⅓ cup crumbled Gorgonzola cheese
⅓ cup dried cranberries
1 pear, cored and cut into thin wedges

*To make the bacon:*

Preheat the oven to 400 degrees. Line a 15 x 10-inch jelly-roll pan with foil and place a baking rack on the pan. Spray the rack with nonstick cooking spray.

Combine the pecans and brown sugar on a plate or in a shallow dish. Pour the maple syrup in another shallow dish. Coat each slice of bacon with the maple syrup and press into the pecan mixture, turning to coat on both sides. Arrange the coated bacon on the rack in the pan.

Bake for 25 to 30 minutes or until crispy. Remove from the oven and stare at this wondrous creation. Let cool for at least 5 minutes to set up before removing from the pan. At this point you can set the bacon aside on a dish and cover loosely with paper towels for up to 2 hours or refrigerate overnight.

*To make the dressing:*

In a jar with a tight-fitting lid, combine the oil, cider and balsamic vinegars, mustard, maple syrup, shallot, salt, and pepper. Shake to combine.

*To assemble the salad:*

Divide the lettuce among four salad plates. Equally distribute the Gorgonzola cheese, cranberries, and pear slices over the lettuce. Crumble 6 slices of the bacon and sprinkle on the salads. Drizzle with the dressing.

NOTE: While I have never seen it happen, I suppose it is possible to have some bacon left over. It will keep up to 4 days in a sealable plastic bag in the refrigerator.

# COLORFUL WALDORF SALAD

*Green and red apples and cranberries are so festive and colorful, and the salad is cool and crunchy, making it the perfect side for a spicy entrée.*

**MAKES 8 SERVINGS.**

**SALAD**

3 green apples, chopped
3 red apples, chopped
Juice of half a lemon
½ cup toasted pecans
½ cup dried cranberries
4 stalks celery, chopped

**DRESSING**

½ cup sour cream
6 tablespoons mayonnaise
1 teaspoon lemon zest
Juice of half a lemon
2 tablespoons firmly packed brown sugar

*To make the salad:*

Combine the apples and the lemon juice in a large bowl. Add the pecans, cranberries, and celery.

*To make the dressing:*

In a medium bowl whisk together the sour cream, mayonnaise, lemon zest, lemon juice, and brown sugar. Stir the dressing into the salad mixture and chill at least 1 hour before serving.

# NEW POTATO SALAD

*It's always a pleasant surprise when I remove the lid to expose my creamy, herb-flavored potato salad instead of the yellow egg, celery, mustard, and relish recipe. I do love the classic, especially with chopped bread and butter pickles, but this version is my favorite. The subtle flavors make the potatoes the star instead of smothering them.*

**MAKES 8 SERVINGS.**

3 pounds new potatoes, skin on

2 teaspoons salt, divided

1 small red onion, peeled

1 cup sour cream

1 cup mayonnaise

2 tablespoons chopped fresh parsley

2 tablespoons chopped chives

1 ½ teaspoons dried tarragon

½ teaspoon black pepper

Wash the potatoes and place in a large pot. Add enough water to completely cover the potatoes. Bring to a boil over high heat. Add 1 teaspoon salt to the water. Reduce temperature to medium-high and boil the potatoes for about 20 minutes or until tender. Drain. Set aside until cool enough to handle but still warm.

Cut the potatoes into halves, or quarters if they are really large. Place in a large bowl. Cut the onion in half and then cut each half into thin slices. Place in the bowl with the potatoes.

In a medium bowl stir together the sour cream, mayonnaise, parsley, chives, tarragon, the remaining 1 teaspoon salt, and pepper until combined. Pour two-thirds of the sauce over the warm potatoes and stir to combine. Cover and refrigerate until chilled, and keep the rest of the sauce in the refrigerator as well.

Before serving, stir the potato salad and add more of the sauce if needed to achieve the desired consistency.

# COLESLAW

*The only coleslaw I will eat is the one my mom made when I was growing up. So, of course, her recipe is the only one I make. I made one tiny change to Mom's recipe by adding a minced shallot. I love this coleslaw so much. It's the perfect cool and creamy partner to spicy barbecue.*

**MAKES 6 TO 8 SERVINGS.**

2 heaping tablespoons mayonnaise

2 tablespoons vegetable oil

4 tablespoons cider vinegar

2 tablespoons sugar

1 shallot, peeled and minced

Salt and black pepper to taste

1 head green cabbage

3 carrots

In a jar with a tight-fitting lid, combine the mayonnaise, oil, vinegar, sugar, and shallot by shaking until smooth. Season with salt and pepper to taste.

Remove the outer leaves from the head of cabbage and then cut into quarters and remove the core. Thinly slice quarters to a shredded consistency and place in a large bowl. Peel the carrots and then grate on a box grater and add to the bowl. Pour the dressing over the cabbage mixture and stir to combine. Cover and let sit in the refrigerator for 1 hour before serving.

# WILD RICE SALAD

*A wonderfully unique salad. Because you make it the day before you serve it, it's great to take to a potluck. It also holds up very well, lasting a few days in the refrigerator without getting mushy like most salads.*

**MAKES 8 TO 10 SERVINGS.**

½ cup extra-virgin olive oil

⅓ cup balsamic vinegar

2 teaspoons Dijon mustard

1 clove garlic, minced

½ teaspoon kosher salt

½ teaspoon fresh ground black pepper

4 green onions, thinly sliced

1 cup uncooked wild rice, prepared as directed on package and cooled

1 Red Delicious apple, cored and chopped

1 Golden Delicious apple, cored and chopped

½ cup dried cranberries

1 tablespoon butter

½ cup chopped walnuts

In a small bowl combine the oil, vinegar, mustard, garlic, salt, and pepper with a whisk. Stir in the onions. In a large bowl combine the prepared rice, apples, and cranberries.

In a small skillet melt the butter over medium heat. Add the walnuts and sauté for 5 minutes, stirring frequently. Add the walnuts to the rice mixture. Pour the dressing over the rice and stir to combine. Cover and refrigerate overnight.

# PRIMAVERA PASTA SALAD

*For about ten years I was asked to bring this salad to every single gathering I was invited to. Everyone raved about it and wanted to know if my amazing salad dressing recipe was a secret or if I was willing to share. Their jaws always dropped when I admitted all I did was mix some mayonnaise and Parmesan cheese into vinaigrette salad dressing.*

**MAKES 10 SERVINGS.**

1 pound tricolored spiral pasta, cooked 1 minute less than directed on the package and drained

3 stalks celery, chopped

2 carrots, peeled and sliced

½ cup frozen baby peas

1 small red onion, finely chopped

1 cup broccoli florets

1 cup large black olives, halved

1 cup cherry or grape tomatoes, halved

1 small zucchini, halved lengthwise, then sliced

1 small yellow squash, halved lengthwise, then sliced

1 ½ cups of your favorite bottled or prepared vinaigrette

½ cup mayonnaise

½ cup shredded Parmesan cheese, plus extra for garnish

Salt and black pepper to taste

Sliced red bell peppers for garnish

Chopped fresh parsley for garnish

Place the pasta in a large bowl while it's still warm and add the celery, carrots, peas, onion, broccoli, olives, tomatoes, zucchini, and squash. Stir to combine. In a small bowl combine the vinaigrette, mayonnaise, and Parmesan cheese. Pour half of the dressing over the salad and stir to combine. Add additional dressing until the desired consistency is reached. Taste and add the salt and pepper, if needed. Cover and refrigerate several hours or overnight.

Before serving, garnish with sliced red peppers, freshly chopped parsley, and extra grated Parmesan cheese (if desired).

# UPSIDE-DOWN CHICKEN PAILLARD SALAD

*When I was growing up we visited the Italian side of the family a couple of times a year, and every single trip included at least one meal of chicken cutlets. They were always served with a green salad with oil and vinegar dressing, and some crusty Italian bread.*

*My upside-down salad stems from these memories. Each bite of my chicken cutlet was always topped with a healthy forkful of salad. I've loved chicken and salad together ever since. When you order a salad with grilled chicken in restaurants, you typically find the strips of chicken placed on top of the salad. Well, since I like my vinegary salad piled on my chicken, I make mine upside down. I listed my favorite salad ingredients, but you can use your own favorites. I didn't list quantity of salad ingredients because it really is up to you. Use as much or as little as you like.*

**MAKES 1 SERVING.**

1 chicken breast

1 tablespoon milk

1 large egg

Italian-style bread crumbs (or Italian-style panko bread crumbs)

Olive oil for skillet

Mixed greens

Grape or cherry tomatoes, cut in half

Cucumber, cut in half and sliced

Red onion, quartered and sliced

Celery, chopped

Black olives, cut in half lengthwise

Your favorite vinaigrette

Shredded Parmesan cheese

Butterfly the chicken breast and then pound thin so the finished cutlet is almost the size of your plate.

In a shallow dish mix the milk into the egg. Pour the bread crumbs into a separate shallow dish. (Amounts of egg and bread crumbs will depend on the amount of chicken you are cooking. Just eyeball it.)

Heat a skillet over medium heat and coat the bottom with olive oil. When the pan is hot, coat each piece of chicken in the egg and then in the bread crumbs. Place in the hot skillet. For thin cutlets, it should take only 3 to 4 minutes per side.

Remove the cooked cutlets to a rack so they stay crispy. When ready to serve, place the chicken on a plate and arrange the mixed greens, tomatoes, cucumber, onion, celery, and olives on top or just to the side of the chicken. Drizzle the chicken and salad with your favorite vinaigrette and sprinkle with Parmesan cheese.

Upside-Down Chicken Paillard Salad (above; page 69)          Grilled Chicken and Berry Salad (below; page 71)

# GRILLED CHICKEN AND BERRY SALAD

*So very easy and definitely pretty enough to serve to company. I grill several chicken breasts at one time and freeze them in individual freezer bags so I can take one out when needed for a quick dinner after work.*

**MAKES 1 SERVING.**

2 cups mixed baby greens

1 grilled chicken breast, sliced

4 strawberries, quartered

¼ cup blueberries

1 tablespoon crumbled Gorgonzola, blue, or goat cheese

2 tablespoons almond slivers, toasted (see note)

2 teaspoons good-quality, low- or no-sugar-added seedless raspberry preserves

4 teaspoons extra-virgin olive oil

2 teaspoons cider vinegar

2 teaspoons balsamic vinegar

Salt and black pepper to taste

Arrange the greens on a dinner plate. Arrange sliced chicken down the center of the greens. Sprinkle the berries, cheese, and almonds on top. In a small bowl combine the preserves, oil, cider and balsamic vinegars, salt, and pepper with a whisk. Drizzle over the salad and serve immediately.

NOTE: To toast almonds, place a skillet over medium heat. Do not spray the skillet or add any oil. Once the skillet is hot, add the almonds in a single layer and cook, stirring frequently, for approximately 5 minutes, or until golden brown.

# PICO DE GALLO SALAD

*The only reason I came up with this salad is because I wanted to pick ingredients I don't like out of pico de gallo, and everything was chopped so finely it was an impossible task. By cutting everything into large chunks and not finely chopping the cilantro (which I don't like at all), I am able to eat around the things I don't like while my friends enjoy all the flavors they love. I like to serve it with fajitas, enchiladas, or any spicy Mexican food. It really brightens up the plate.*

**MAKES 8 SERVINGS.**

6 Roma tomatoes, quartered

1 medium red onion, chopped

1 avocado, peeled and cut into bite-size cubes

1 jalapeño pepper, seeded and finely chopped

2 limes

2 tablespoons extra-virgin olive oil

1 tablespoon white vinegar

½ teaspoon salt

¼ teaspoon black pepper

1 teaspoon sugar

⅓ cup fresh cilantro leaves, very roughly chopped

Combine the tomatoes, onion, avocado, and jalapeño in a large bowl. Zest 1 lime and set the zest aside. Juice both limes into a small bowl. Add the olive oil, vinegar, salt, pepper, sugar, and lime zest. Whisk to combine and drizzle over the tomato mixture. Toss to combine. Add the cilantro and gently stir. Chill for 1 hour before serving.

# SOUPS AND SANDWICHES

## COZY COMFORT

"I am the bread of life. Whoever comes to me will never go
hungry, and whoever believes in me will never be thirsty."

—JOHN 6:35

On a cold winter's night, a steamy bowl of soup and a grilled cheese sandwich can warm you down to your toes. Soups are almost impossible to mess up, and putting cheese between two slices of bread before grilling to golden buttery goodness is never a bad thing. That makes this winning combination perfect for beginner cooks. And because mixing and matching soups and sandwiches gives you endless lunch and dinner possibilities, you will never tire of this comforting duo.

## SOUPS

Split Pea Soup

Chicken and Harvest Vegetable Soup

Butternut Squash Bisque

Roasted Tomato Bisque

Loaded Baked Potato Soup

NaNa's Hearty Bean Soup

Crab and Corn Chowder

## SANDWICHES

Grilled Cheese and Paninis

Patty Melt

Grilled Chicken Parmesan Sandwich

Sloppy Joes

Slow-Cooker Barbecue

Cranberry Chicken Salad Sandwich

# SOUPS

On rainy Sunday afternoons there's nothing I enjoy more than wrapping my hands around a warm mug of soup. I look for an old musical on television, curl up on the couch with a blanket, and sip soup from a mug. I never quite make it to the end of the movie, though. As soon as the warm soup hits my tummy, I'm in La-La Land. Ahhhh . . .

## SPLIT PEA SOUP

*When the temperatures dip into the teens and my house looks like an igloo, I want soup! During a rare snowbound weekend I made a pot of my healthy pea soup. My house smelled warm and inviting as the soup simmered on the stove. Too bad you needed an icepick to get to my front door.*

*To minimize the fat content without losing the smoky flavor, I used a smoked turkey wing instead of a ham hock. You won't be able to tell the difference.*

---

**MAKES 6 TO 8 SERVINGS.**

1 smoked turkey wing or drumstick

1 pound dried split peas, rinsed and drained

1 onion, finely chopped

4 to 5 carrots, peeled, sliced in half lengthwise, and chopped

5 celery stalks with leaves, chopped

2 to 3 cloves garlic, minced

¼ cup chopped fresh Italian flat-leaf parsley

2 teaspoons dried thyme

1 teaspoon sea salt

1 teaspoon black pepper

10 cups water

2 bay leaves

Throw everything into the large pot. Yes, it really is that easy! Bring to a boil. Reduce heat, cover loosely, and simmer for 1 hour.

Remove the turkey and set aside until cool enough to handle. Remove the skin and cut up the meat. Discard the bones and the skin. Return the meat to the pot. Remove the bay leaves and discard.

Ladle a big ol' helping into a bowl.

Eat.

Lick the bowl.

# CHICKEN AND HARVEST VEGETABLE SOUP

*I make this soup whenever I feel like I've been eating too much junk. It's filled with yummy root vegetables, making it very hearty and filling without adding noodles or rice. You can adjust this recipe to suit your own taste. Add your favorite veggies and leave out the ones you don't like. It's your pot! Fill it with the flavors that make you happy.*

**MAKES 6 TO 8 SERVINGS.**

1 chicken, cut into pieces

Water

2 leeks, cut in half and then sliced

2 to 4 carrots, cut into ½-inch pieces

2 to 3 stalks celery (including leaves), cut into ½-inch pieces

2 sweet potatoes, peeled and cut into bite-size cubes

1 rutabaga, peeled and cut into bite-size cubes

2 to 3 parsnips, peeled, cut in half, and sliced into ½-inch pieces

1 ½ cups cubed butternut squash

1 (8-ounce) package sliced fresh mushrooms

1 (5-ounce) bag spinach leaves

½ cup fresh Italian flat-leaf parsley

1 ½ teaspoons dried thyme

1 teaspoon salt

1 teaspoon black pepper

Grated Parmesan cheese for serving

Place the chicken in a large pot and cover with water. Bring to a boil over medium-high heat, and then reduce heat to medium or medium-low until you have a gentle simmer. Simmer for 45 minutes or until the chicken is cooked through.

Remove the chicken and set aside to cool. Cover the pot and turn off the heat.

When the chicken is cool enough to handle, remove the skin and bones. Place the bones back in the pot and bring to a gentle simmer over medium-high heat. (This extra step will help flavor the stock and give you a good base for your soup.) Cover and simmer on low for 30 minutes. Remove the lid and continue simmering for another 30 minutes.

Shred the chicken while the stock is simmering. Remove the bones from the stock and discard. Add the leeks, carrots, celery, sweet potatoes, rutabaga, parsnips, butternut squash, and mushrooms to the stock. Continue to simmer for 20 to 30 minutes or until the vegetables are tender.

Add the shredded chicken, spinach, parsley, thyme, salt, and pepper. Simmer for 20 minutes. Taste and add more seasoning if desired.

Serve with a little grated Parmesan cheese, if desired.

# BUTTERNUT SQUASH BISQUE

*Because this soup is pureed you can eat it out of a bowl with a spoon or you can pour servings into mugs so you can curl up with a mugful and your favorite blankie. I vote for mug and blankie.*

**MAKES 6 SERVINGS.**

5 strips bacon, cut into thin slices

2 leeks, white part only, cut in half lengthwise and sliced

2 cloves garlic, minced

3 cups cubed butternut squash

1 cup peeled and cubed Yukon Gold or red potatoes

4 cups vegetable stock

1 cup pumpkin puree

½ cup heavy cream

⅓ cup dry sherry

2 tablespoons chopped fresh sage

½ teaspoon ground ginger

Salt and black pepper to taste

Dash cayenne pepper (or more to taste)

Whole sage leaves for garnish, if desired

Heat a large pot over medium-high heat. Add the bacon, stirring to separate the pieces as it cooks. When the bacon is crisp, remove with a slotted spoon to a paper towel to drain, leaving the bacon grease in the pot.

Add the leeks to the bacon fat. Ohhhhh . . . something magical happens the moment the leeks hit the bacon grease. Can't you just smell the goodness? Sauté the leeks for about 5 minutes, stirring occasionally. Add the garlic and continue to cook for 1 minute.

Add the squash and potatoes to the pan, stirring to coat with the pan drippings and leeks. Stir in the vegetable stock and bring to a simmer. Simmer for 30 to 40 minutes or until the vegetables are fork-tender. Remove the pot from the heat.

Let the soup cool for about 15 minutes. (You can also prepare up to this point the day before you want to serve. Simply cover and refrigerate.)

Puree the vegetables until smooth using an immersion or standard blender. (If using a standard blender and the soup is hot, puree in batches, not filling the blender more than halfway full to avoid messy explosions.)

Bring the soup to a simmer over low to medium-low heat and add the pumpkin, cream, and sherry. Simmer for 5 minutes and then stir in the sage and ginger. Taste before adding salt, pepper, and cayenne.

Serve with the reserved bacon bits and garnish with sage leaves.

**HEALTHY VARIATIONS:** Skip the bacon. Sauté the leeks in a little olive oil (just enough to coat the bottom of your pot) before proceeding with the rest of recipe. You can also replace the heavy cream with evaporated milk.

**FLAVOR VARIATIONS:** You can give this a Latin twist by adding cumin instead of ginger and sage, and then top with roasted pumpkin seeds. You can use sweet potatoes instead of regular potatoes and add cinnamon and nutmeg along with the ginger and skip the sage. Curry would be another good flavor for this type of root vegetable puree.

# ROASTED TOMATO BISQUE

*I grew up on canned tomato soup made with milk and grilled cheese sandwiches made with single-wrapped cheese slices. While I still enjoy the canned stuff my mom made, I love homemade tomato soup and grilled cheese sandwiches or paninis made with a variety of cheeses and fillings. Mozzarella and pesto grilled cheese is especially good with this soup.*

*Roasting the tomatoes and vegetables brings out their sweetness. It's an extra step but definitely worth it.*

**MAKES 8 SERVINGS.**

6 Roma tomatoes, seeded and quartered

1 (28-ounce) can whole, peeled San Marzano tomatoes, drained with juice reserved (use canned whole plum tomatoes if you can't find San Marzano)

1 onion, peeled, halved, and sliced

2 leeks, white part only, sliced

1 stalk celery with leaves, cut into ½-inch slices

1 carrot, peeled and cut into ½-inch rounds

5 cloves garlic, peeled

¼ cup extra-virgin olive oil

1 teaspoon salt

1 teaspoon black pepper

3 cups vegetable or chicken stock, divided

½ teaspoon dried thyme

1 cup heavy cream

6 basil leaves, torn

Preheat the oven to 400 degrees. Line a 15 x 10-inch jelly-roll pan with parchment paper. Arrange fresh and drained tomatoes, onions, leeks, celery, carrots, and garlic in a single layer on the jelly-roll pan. (If they don't fit in a single layer, use a second pan.) Drizzle with the olive oil and sprinkle with salt and pepper.

Roast in the oven for 30 minutes or until the vegetables are brown at the edges, stirring once after 15 minutes. Keep the vegetables in a single layer so they caramelize.

Remove the roasted vegetables from the oven and let cool for 15 minutes. Transfer to a pot along with any accumulated juices. Add the reserved tomato juice and 1 cup of the stock. Use an immersion blender to puree the vegetables or puree them in batches in a blender, making sure not to fill blender more than halfway full with each batch.

Add the remaining 2 cups stock and thyme. Bring to a simmer over medium-low heat and cook, stirring occasionally, for 10 minutes. Add the cream and warm just to boiling point. Taste and adjust seasoning if necessary.

Serve garnished with basil.

# LOADED BAKED POTATO SOUP

*Everything you would pile on top of a baked potato in a bowl. Love in a bowl.*

**MAKES 8 SERVINGS.**

½ pound bacon, cut into 1-inch pieces

1 yellow onion, chopped

2 medium leeks, white part only, chopped

2 stalks celery with leaves, chopped

2 carrots, peeled and chopped

10 large Yukon Gold potatoes, peeled and cut into large cubes

6 cups chicken stock

½ cup chopped fresh Italian flat-leaf parsley

1 teaspoon salt

½ teaspoon ground black pepper

¼ teaspoon cayenne pepper (or to taste)

4 ounces cream cheese, cut into cubes, softened

1 cup heavy cream

2 cups shredded Cheddar cheese, divided

2 tablespoons fresh chopped chives

3 green onions, chopped

Cook the bacon in a large pot over medium heat. When the bacon is crispy, remove to drain on paper towels. Add the onions, leeks, celery, and carrots to the bacon grease and sauté for 5 minutes. Add the potatoes and stock and bring to a simmer. If the potatoes are not completely covered in stock, add more stock or water until just covered. Bring to a boil. Reduce the heat to medium and simmer for 20 minutes or until the potatoes are tender.

Remove the pan from the heat and let cool for 15 minutes. Use an immersion blender to puree the soup, or puree in batches in a blender, being careful not to fill blender more than halfway full with each batch.

Add the parsley, salt, pepper, and cayenne and taste for seasoning, adding more if needed. Stir in the cream cheese, cream, and 1 cup of the shredded Cheddar cheese. Place over low heat and stir until the cheese is melted.

Serve garnished with additional cheese, chives, green onions, and the reserved bacon.

*Let go of perfect. There is just as much love around a scratched-up kitchen table as there is around a table covered in a beautiful linen tablecloth.*

# NANA'S HEARTY BEAN SOUP

*I remember my NaNa putting together bags or jars of mixed dried beans as Christmas gifts. She added her Good Luck New Year's Soup recipe tied on with a pretty bow. I kept a bag of her soup mix and her recipe for about ten years just because NaNa had made it. I didn't make the soup until after she died—with fresh beans, of course. I put the beans from NaNa's mix in a glass jar and kept it on my kitchen counter so she was always in the kitchen with me. This is her recipe. I have found that grandmothers always know best.*

**MAKES 8 SERVINGS.**

1 (16-ounce) bag mixed dried beans
1 tablespoon plus 1 teaspoon salt, divided
2 quarts water
1 large smoked ham hock
½ cup barley
3 stalks celery with leaves, chopped
2 carrots, peeled and chopped
1 (28-ounce) can diced tomatoes with juice
1 large onion, chopped
3 cloves garlic, minced
Juice of 1 lemon
1 teaspoon chili powder
½ teaspoon ground cumin
½ teaspoon crushed dried thyme
1 teaspoon sugar
½ teaspoon black pepper
½ cup chopped fresh parsley

Place the beans in a colander and rinse with cool water. Drain and transfer the beans to a large pot. Cover with water and add 1 tablespoon salt. Cover pot and place in the refrigerator to soak overnight. Drain the soaked beans and rinse in a colander.

*continued on next page*

Rinse out the pot and transfer the drained and rinsed beans back into the pot. Add 2 quarts water, the ham hock, and barley. Bring to a boil over medium-high heat and cover, leaving the lid off to the side so there is a little space for steam to escape. Reduce the heat to low and simmer for about 2 hours or until the beans are just about cooked. Remove the ham hock and set aside.

Add the celery, carrots, tomatoes with juices, onions, garlic, lemon juice, chili powder, cumin, thyme, sugar, and pepper, and simmer for 30 to 40 minutes or until the vegetables are tender. While the vegetables are cooking, remove the meat from the ham hock and return the meat to the soup. Discard the bones. Stir in the parsley right before serving.

# CRAB AND CORN CHOWDER

*This soup is wonderful when corn is in season. The sweetness of the corn and the crab works wonderfully with the hint of cayenne.*

**MAKES 8 SERVINGS.**

6 ears corn

5 cups vegetable or chicken stock

3 cups heavy cream

2 bay leaves

½ pound bacon, cut into 1-inch pieces

2 onions, chopped

1 small red bell pepper, seeded and finely chopped

2 stalks celery with leaves, chopped

1 large carrot, peeled and diced

1 ½ teaspoon salt

1 pound small red potatoes

1 ½ tablespoons chopped fresh chives

1 teaspoon thyme dried leaves

Dash of cayenne pepper

⅓ cup chopped fresh Italian flat-leaf parsley

1 pound fresh lump crabmeat

Cut the corn from the cobs, set the corn aside, and place cobs in a large pot. Pour the stock and cream over the cobs. Add the bay leaves and place over medium heat. Simmer for 5 minutes. Remove from the heat.

In a heavy skillet, cook the bacon until crispy. Remove the bacon with a slotted spoon to paper towels to drain. Add the onions, red peppers, celery, and carrots to the bacon grease and sauté for 5 minutes.

Remove the cobs and bay leaves from the pot and discard. Use a slotted spoon to transfer the sautéed vegetables to the pot. Add the salt and potatoes and simmer for 10 to 15 minutes or until the potatoes are just tender. Add the fresh corn kernels, chives, thyme, and cayenne. Taste and adjust seasoning if needed. Simmer for 5 minutes. Stir in the parsley and crabmeat just to heat through, and then remove the pot from the heat and serve sprinkled with the cooked bacon.

# SANDWICHES

Sandwiches were a staple in our house when I was growing up. There was always a sandwich in our lunchbox and sandwiches for lunch on weekends. Bologna on white bread, peanut butter and jelly, grilled cheese, and tuna salad sandwiches are what I remember most. I was always pretty excited when Mom made fried bologna sandwiches, as they were not in our normal sandwich rotation.

I still love sandwiches, but not the sandwiches I grew up with. My palate has definitely changed. I had my fill of lunchbox sandwiches years ago. Now I prefer my sandwiches grilled or pressed or on a crusty roll, with gooey cheese oozing out between slices of buttery grilled bread.

You can make a sandwich out of just about anything. A sandwich makes any meal portable so you can eat on the go. I've even seen people put leftover cold lasagna or spaghetti in between two slices of bread. I would say, "Eww," but I'm not one to judge.

The creation of the perfect sandwich is an art form. Be creative. Think outside the box . . . er . . . the white bread.

NOTE: If you have never had a fried bologna sandwich, you need to make one immediately. Don't be a skeptic. Don't turn your nose up in the air. Just make one. Cut about 3 slits around the edges of 2 slices of bologna. Fry in butter in a skillet until the edges are brown. Toast 2 slices of bread. Spread plain yellow mustard on 1 slice. Top with fried bologna, then crispy iceberg lettuce. Spread mayonnaise on the other slice of toast and close your sandwich. Cut in half diagonally (because that's the way my mom cut them) and sink your teeth into this classic Southern yumminess. OK, now you can turn up your nose . . . but only if your opinion hasn't changed.

# GRILLED CHEESE AND PANINIS

*The only real difference in a grilled cheese sandwich and a panini is that paninis are pressed, cooking on both sides at the same time. I also make wraps using the same technique I use to make paninis.*

### TO MAKE A GRILLED CHEESE:

Butter the outside of each slice of bread. Add the fillings of your choice to the unbuttered sides, making sure the cheese is closest to the bread. Close the sandwich and place on a hot griddle or skillet over medium heat. Cook until golden, and then turn over. Remove from the pan when golden on both sides and the cheese has melted.

### TO MAKE A PANINI:

Butter the outside of each slice of bread or lightly brush with extra-virgin olive oil. Add the fillings of your choice to the unbuttered side of one of the slices. Then top with the other slice of bread, butter side out. Place in a panini press and cook until golden on both sides. If you don't have a panini press, place the sandwich in a heavy skillet or on a ridged griddle. Place a heavy skillet or a foil-wrapped brick on top of the sandwich. When the bottom of the sandwich is golden, turn over and return the heavy skillet or brick to the top to press the sandwich. Remove when the second side is golden and the filling is hot.

### TO MAKE A WRAP:

Fill a tortilla or any flavor wrap with the fillings of your choice, roll the tortilla burrito-style, coat the outside with butter or oil, and cook as directed for paninis.

### My favorite breads for grilled, pressed, or wrapped sandwiches:

Rustic country bread

Ciabatta

Sourdough

Marble rye

Croissant

Sandwich or submarine roll

French baguette

Spinach wrap

### My favorite filling combinations:

**French Onion Soup**

> Caramelized onions with thyme
> Gruyere cheese
> Thinly sliced roast beef (optional)

**Italian Flag**

> Roasted red pepper
> Spinach
> Smoked Provolone cheese
> Fresh basil leaves

**Bacon and Cheddar (really good on rustic sourdough)**

> Cheddar cheese
> Bacon, cooked until crispy
> Thinly sliced tomatoes

**Reuben (use marble rye bread)**

> Corned beef or pastrami
> Gruyere or Swiss cheese
> Whole grain mustard
> Sauerkraut

**Roast Beef**

> Thinly sliced deli roast beef
> Garlic and herb cream cheese or goat cheese spread
> Provolone cheese
> Sliced tomatoes
> Fresh basil leaves

**Apricot Turkey**

> Turkey slices
> Havarti cheese
> Apricot preserves

**Turkey and Cranberry**

> Turkey slices
> Cream cheese
> Cranberry chutney

**Caprese**

> Mozzarella cheese
> Tomato slices
> Pesto sauce

**Gourmet Ham and Cheese**

> Sliced ham
> Brie cheese
> Thinly sliced apples

**French Dip**

> Beef
> Provolone cheese
> Caramelized onions
> Sautéed mushrooms
> Au jus sauce for dipping

# PATTY MELT

*Patty melts are a heavenly combination of a juicy bacon burger and a grilled cheese sandwich. What's not to love about that?!*

**MAKES 1 SERVING.**

2 tablespoons butter, softened
Whole grain country mustard
2 slices marble rye bread
2 slices Swiss cheese
Cooked hamburger patty
3 slices cooked bacon
Caramelized onions (recipe follows)

Add 1 tablespoon of butter to a heavy skillet and place over medium heat.

Spread the mustard on one side of each slice of bread. Place 1 slice of cheese over the mustard on both pieces of bread. Add the burger to one slice, arrange bacon and caramelized onions on the burger, and top with second slice to form a sandwich. Spread the remaining butter on the outside of both sides of the sandwich.

Place the sandwich in the skillet and cook until golden. Turn over and continue cooking until golden and the cheese has melted. Remove from the skillet, cut in half, and serve immediately.

**CARAMELIZED ONIONS**

2 onions
2 tablespoons butter
3 tablespoons brown sugar

Cut the onions in half, and thinly slice. Add the butter to a skillet and place over medium heat. Add onions and sauté for 5 minutes. Sprinkle onions with brown sugar. Stir to coat onions. Reduce heat to low and sauté, stirring occasionally, for 30 minutes or until onions are a deep golden brown.

> *Creating unforgettable meals for the special people in your life begins and ends with love.*

# GRILLED CHICKEN PARMESAN SANDWICH

*Chicken Parmesan is one of my favorite dishes and one I usually order when I go to an Italian restaurant. This is my sandwich version. If you keep grilled chicken breasts in your freezer, once you thaw the chicken you can have this ready in about fifteen minutes. Great for busy weeknights!*

**MAKES 1 SERVING.**

1 ciabatta roll

1 tablespoon butter, softened

½ clove garlic, minced

1 tablespoon Parmesan cheese

½ cup marinara sauce

1 grilled chicken breast

Sliced Provolone or mozzarella cheese

2 to 3 fresh basil leaves, optional

Roasted red bell peppers, optional

Move the oven rack to the second position from the top and preheat the broiler.

Split the ciabatta roll. In a small bowl combine the butter with the garlic and Parmesan cheese and spread on the inside of the ciabatta roll. Place the bottom half of the roll butter side up on a cookie sheet and place under the broiler for 2 minutes or until golden brown.

Remove from the oven and spread with a few spoonsful of the marinara sauce. Place the chicken breast on the sauce and top with the Provolone cheese. Add the top half of the bun, butter side up, to the cookie sheet beside the bottom half and return the pan to the oven under the broiler for 1 to 2 minutes. Remove when the cheese has melted and the top half is golden.

Spread a few spoonsful of marinara sauce on the top half of the roll. If using basil leaves and roasted red peppers, add them now. If not, put the top half of the roll on top of the cheese and serve immediately with a side salad drizzled with Italian dressing.

> *There is always room for one more plate, one more chair, one more hungry soul at the table.*

# SLOPPY JOES

*You can make a batch of sloppy joe filling a day or two ahead and keep it in the refrigerator for a fast weeknight family dinner. All you have to do is reheat the filling and prepare the buns. Dinner will be on the table in fifteen minutes! Eating sloppy sloppy joes is a great family bonding experience. The bigger the mess, the bigger the laughs.*

**MAKES 8 SERVINGS.**

2.5 pounds ground sirloin

1 medium onion, chopped

1 green bell pepper, seeded and very finely chopped

4 cloves garlic, minced

1 (8-ounce) can tomato sauce

2 tablespoons tomato paste

2 tablespoons Worcestershire sauce

2 tablespoons cider vinegar

3 teaspoons prepared mustard

3 tablespoons firmly packed brown sugar

1 teaspoon kosher or sea salt

½ teaspoon black pepper

A couple dashes of cayenne pepper (or more to taste)

8 slices Cheddar cheese

8 sesame seed buns

2 tablespoons butter, softened

Heat a large skillet over medium heat. Add the ground sirloin to the hot skillet and brown, stirring frequently, as you break up the clumps of meat. When the meat is almost cooked, add the onion, green pepper, and garlic. Continue cooking until the meat is cooked through.

Stir in the tomato sauce, tomato paste, Worcestershire, vinegar, mustard, brown sugar, salt, pepper, and cayenne. Simmer for 20 minutes or until thickened.

Preheat the broiler.

Place a slice of cheese on the bottom half of each bun. Lightly butter the top half. Place under the broiler and broil until the cheese is melted and the top half is golden. (This will only take a few minutes, so keep a close eye on them.)

To serve, spoon the meat mixture on the bottom half of the bun, and top with the toasted half. I know it seems odd to put the cheese on the bottom, but it helps keep the meat mixture from dripping through the bun while it's on your plate. Although that would make them sloppier!

# SLOW-COOKER BARBECUE

*Here in the South we take our barbecue very seriously. Heated competitions are held throughout the summer months, with grill masters proudly presenting their smoky offerings to the judging panel and to hungry, drooling guests. At the risk of being branded a Yankee, I present my Slow-Cooker Barbecue for those of us without a pit in our backyard. It won't win a grill master contest, but I guarantee it will bring a tear to your eye.*

**MAKES 10 SERVINGS.**

2 medium yellow onions, peeled, cut in half, then sliced

3-pound chuck beef or pork roast

2 (18-ounce) bottles barbecue sauce

1 or 2 jalapeño peppers (if you like spicy barbecue)

10 toasted sesame seed buns

Coleslaw (recipe on page 66), for serving

Onion strings (recipe follows), for serving

Place half of the onions in the bottom of a slow cooker. Lay the roast over the onions and top with the remaining onions. Pour the barbecue sauce over the onions. If using jalapeños, cut in half and scrape out the seeds. Tuck them around the roast.

Cover and cook on low for 8 hours or until the meat falls apart easily.

Remove the meat from the slow cooker and place on a large cutting board. Use two forks to shred the meat. Spoon enough of the barbecue sauce over the meat to moisten.

Serve shredded meat on toasted sesame seed buns with coleslaw and onion strings, if desired.

**ONION STRINGS**

Vegetable oil for frying

2 onions or 5 to 6 shallots

½ cup all-purpose flour

½ teaspoon salt

¼ teaspoon black pepper

Place a heavy skillet over medium-high heat and fill with oil to ½ inch deep. Bring oil to 375 degrees. (If you don't have a thermometer, you can test the oil by dropping a pinch of flour into the oil. If it sizzles, the oil is hot enough.)

While the oil heats, peel and thinly slice the onions or shallots.

In a shallow dish combine the flour, salt, and pepper. Add the onions or shallots, breaking into pieces as you toss to coat.

Shake off excess flour as you drop the onions into the hot oil. Fry until crispy, stirring gently only as needed to keep from burning. Drain on paper towels.

# CRANBERRY CHICKEN SALAD SANDWICH

*This is a little different from traditional chicken salad recipes. The toasted pecans add a wonderful flavor and texture, and the cranberries are a nice burst of brightness. It can also be served on a bed of lettuce with a colorful fruit salad on the side.*

**MAKES 10 TO 14 SANDWICHES.**

4 cups cooked, chopped skinless chicken breast meat

3 green onions, chopped

3 to 4 stalks celery, cut in half lengthwise and chopped

⅔ cup chopped pecans, toasted and cooled

⅔ cup dried cranberries

½ cup mayonnaise

½ cup sour cream

1 ½ teaspoons dried tarragon

½ teaspoon salt

½ teaspoon black pepper

To make sandwich:

Makes 1 serving.

2 slices of hearty whole grain bread

3 tablespoons cream cheese, softened

Lettuce leaves

Alfalfa sprouts

3 tablespoons whole berry cranberry sauce

Combine the chicken, onions, celery, pecans, and cranberries in a large bowl. In a medium bowl combine the mayonnaise, sour cream, tarragon, salt, and pepper. Stir the dressing into the chicken. Cover and store in the refrigerator for 2 hours or overnight.

*continued on next page*

When ready to make sandwich, toast the bread and spread one side of each slice with the cream cheese. Spoon the chicken salad over one slice of the bread. Top with lettuce and sprouts. Spoon whole berry cranberry sauce over the cream cheese on the other slice of bread; then place, cranberry sauce side down, on top of the lettuce and spouts. Delicious!

NOTE: For a beautiful shower appetizer, spread chicken salad on spinach flatbread, roll it up into a long cylinder, cut into 1-inch spirals, and arrange on a pretty serving dish. Or spoon into individual cooked tartlet shells and garnish with a little bit of alfalfa sprouts, dried cranberries, or fresh tarragon. Gorgeous!

> *Cheerfully share your home with those who need a meal or a place to stay. God has given each of you a gift from his great variety of spiritual gifts. Use them well to serve one another.*
>
> —1 PETER 4:9–10 NLT

# ENTRÉES

*Every lesson I learned as a kid was at the dinner table. Being Greek, Sicilian,
and Ruthenian—we are an emotional bunch. It is where we laughed, cried, and
yelled—but most importantly, where we bonded and connected.*
—MICHAEL SYMON

The kitchen table is the anchor of the home. It's where we reconnect with each other in the evenings, encouraging and supporting each other as we share the events of the day. We experience the truest sense of home every time we pull up a chair. With today's hectic pace, the family table is splintering. But what if we slow down and intentionally carve out at least one weeknight to sit together to share a meal with the people we love the most? Let's get back to the family table and reconnect with, encourage, laugh, and love each other as we linger over the last strands of spaghetti.

## BEEF AND PORK

Southern-Style Beef Tips over Rice

Oven-Baked BBQ Beef Short Ribs

Italian Meatloaf

Old-Fashioned Beef and Noodles

Granddaddy's Spicy Stew Meat

Sunday Pork Roast

Low and Slow Pork and Apples

## CHICKEN

Perfect Roast Chicken with Potatoes

Crispy Southern Fried Chicken

Crunchy Herbed Chicken

Chicken Marsala

## SEAFOOD

Pistachio-Crusted Salmon with
Creamy Dijon Sauce

Tequila Shrimp Skewers

Sea Bass with Berry-Mango Salsa

Pan-Seared Scallops on a Bed of
Spinach with Orange Butter Sauce

Lemon Herb-Crusted Fish Fillets

## CASSEROLES

Hot Chicken Salad Casserole

Chicken and Rice Casserole

Whole Wheat Baked Penne
with Vegetables

Easy Chicken Enchiladas

Fiesta Noodle Bake

## PASTA

Lasagna Pinwheels

Shrimp Scampi

Sausage and Pepper Linguine

Pasta in Creamy Savory
Pumpkin Sauce

Linguine with Clam Sauce

## VEGETARIAN

Baked Tortellini

Poblano Popper Stuffed Portobellos

Roasted Veggie Flatbread Pizza

# SOUTHERN-STYLE BEEF TIPS OVER RICE

*I have a thing about rice and brown gravy. Something special happens when you spoon rich beef gravy over rice. It's like happiness on a fork. It's one of my favorite comfort foods.*

*This is a great recipe to bring to a potluck or to someone in need of a hot meal. It reheats well, so you can make it ahead of time. Remember to save a little bit for yourself so you too can experience happiness on a fork.*

*WARNING: Your house will smell amazing, and you may experience a lack of patience as you wait for this dish to be ready.*

**MAKES 6 TO 8 SERVINGS.**

3 pounds beef tips or stew meat

Salt and black pepper

1 onion, peeled and chopped

1 (8-ounce) package sliced fresh mushrooms

1 green bell pepper, seeded and chopped

1 (10.5-ounce) can cream of mushroom soup

1 (1-ounce) package onion soup mix

2 tablespoons Worcestershire sauce

3 cloves garlic, minced

½ cup white wine

1 ½ cups beef broth

6 cups hot, cooked rice for serving

Season the beef with salt and pepper and place in a casserole dish or a slow cooker. Top with the onions, mushrooms, and green peppers.

In a medium bowl whisk together the cream of mushroom soup, onion soup mix, Worcestershire, and garlic until smooth. Whisk in the wine and beef broth until combined, and pour over the beef. Cover the casserole dish tightly or place the lid on the slow cooker.

Bake at 300 degrees for 4 hours or, if using the slow cooker, cook on low for 8 to 9 hours.

Serve over hot, cooked rice.

NOTE: If you prefer a thicker gravy, after the beef has cooked, melt 2 tablespoons butter in a saucepan over medium heat. Add 2 tablespoons all-purpose flour and cook and stir for 1 minute. Slowly whisk in ½ cup of the cooking liquid until smooth. Add another cup and stir until smooth. Add the remaining cooking liquid. (You don't have to drain the meat—just ladle out a good portion of it.) Simmer the gravy for a couple of minutes or until thickened. Add back to the meat and serve.

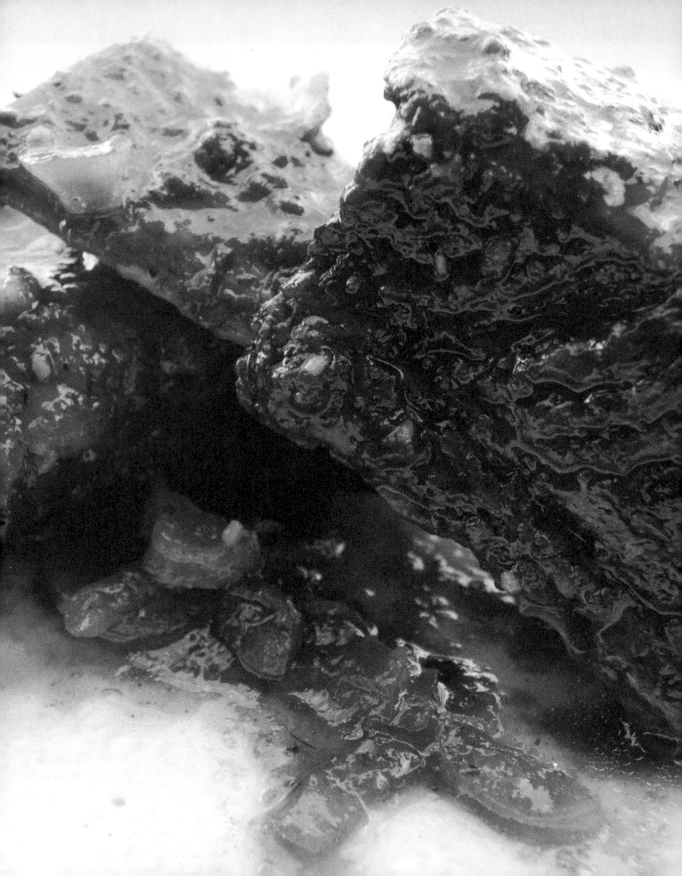

# OVEN-BAKED BBQ BEEF SHORT RIBS

*The only way to cook short ribs is low and slow. My favorite liquids for braising them are marinara sauce, a wine-infused beef broth with onions, and barbecue sauce, as I've done here. The ribs are smothered with onions and barbecue sauce, then slow cooked in the oven. The result is seriously mouthwatering. They are delicious on their own with a crusty piece of bread to sop up the glorious sauce or on a bed of cheesy grits (see page 176 for the recipe). You'll want to make these immediately. Seriously. Go to the grocery store and get the short ribs right now. Don't wait. The tender, falling-apart deliciousness is waiting for you.*

**MAKES 8 SERVINGS.**

4 to 5 pounds boneless or bone-in beef short ribs

Salt, pepper, and garlic powder to season ribs

2 onions, cut in half and then sliced

1 cup ketchup

1 cup firmly packed light brown sugar

1 ½ teaspoons paprika

3 cloves garlic, minced

1 tablespoon cider vinegar

½ teaspoon dried thyme leaves

1 tablespoon spicy brown mustard

2 tablespoons Worcestershire sauce

Preheat the oven to 300 degrees. Arrange the ribs in a large, shallow casserole dish. Season both sides generously with salt, pepper, and garlic powder. Arrange the onions over the ribs.

In a medium bowl combine the ketchup, brown sugar, paprika, minced garlic, vinegar, thyme, mustard, and Worcestershire. Pour over the ribs and onions, and then get your hands in there and make sure the ribs are coated all over with the sauce.

Wash your hands. If you don't, your nose will itch but your hands will be covered in barbecue sauce so you won't be able to scratch. (You know I'm right.)

Tightly cover the dish with foil and roast until the meat is very tender and will fall apart if you poke at it with your fork. This should take about 2 ½ hours. Remove the foil and cook for 30 minutes longer. Let sit for about 30 minutes before serving.

Have I mentioned how mouthwatering these are?

# ITALIAN MEATLOAF

*An Italian twist on an American classic! I make a traditional meatball mixture, pat it into a rectangle, cover with cheese, then roll up and smother in marinara sauce. After baking, I slice it into spirals to reveal swirls of melted cheese and serve with pasta. If you like spaghetti and meatballs, you will love this!*

**MAKES 8 SERVINGS.**

2 pounds ground beef or meatloaf mix (beef, pork, and veal)

2 large eggs

2 tablespoons water

¾ cup Italian-style bread crumbs

⅔ cup grated Parmesan cheese

⅓ cup finely chopped onion

1 teaspoon dried basil leaves

1 teaspoon salt

½ teaspoon black pepper

⅓ cup Italian flat-leaf chopped parsley

3 cloves garlic, minced

3 cups shredded mozzarella or Provolone cheese, divided

1 (24-ounce) jar marinara sauce

Preheat the oven to 350 degrees. Spray a 9 x 13-inch casserole dish with nonstick cooking spray.

In a large bowl combine the ground beef, eggs, water, bread crumbs, Parmesan cheese, onion, basil, salt, pepper, parsley, and garlic until all ingredients are completely incorporated into the beef. Turn out the mixture onto a sheet of waxed paper and shape into an 11 x 9-inch rectangle. Spread 2 cups of the shredded cheese over the meat, leaving a 1-inch border.

Starting at the 9-inch side, roll the meat jelly-roll fashion, lifting the waxed paper as you go to help keep the roll firm. Discard the waxed paper and carefully place the meatloaf, seam side down, into the casserole dish.

Bake for 30 minutes. Pour the marinara sauce over the meatloaf and continue baking for 30 minutes. Sprinkle with the remaining cup of cheese and bake an additional 30 minutes. Remove from the oven and let stand for 15 minutes before slicing.

*Life is about sharing grace, love, and joy and celebrating the here and now.*

# OLD-FASHIONED BEEF AND NOODLES

A big bowl of beef and noodles will warm your tummy and your soul. As it cooks, your house will be filled with the most wonderful, inviting aroma.

Serve with a green salad and crusty whole grain bread for a complete warm-your-tummy, feed-your-soul Sunday supper! Invite some friends or a group of hungry strangers. It will make everyone's tummy happy!

**MAKES 6 SERVINGS.**

2 tablespoons oil (and more as needed)
1 ½ cups all-purpose flour
1 teaspoon salt
1 teaspoon black pepper
1 teaspoon garlic powder
2 pounds stew meat
2 onions, halved and thinly sliced
2 cloves garlic, minced
1 teaspoon dried oregano
1 cup beef broth
1 (8-ounce) package sliced fresh mushrooms
1 ½ cups hot water
8 ounces egg or whole grain noodles, uncooked
⅓ cup fresh chopped Italian flat-leaf parsley for garnish

Coat the bottom of a Dutch oven or large pot with oil. Place over medium-high heat.

In a shallow dish season the flour with the salt, pepper, and garlic powder. Dredge the pieces of stew meat in the seasoned flour and brown in batches in the hot oil. Do not overcrowd in the pan. Remove and set aside as each batch browns. Add oil as needed in between batches.

*continued on next page*

After all of the meat has been browned, reduce the heat to medium and add the onions to the skillet, stirring to coat with pan drippings. Add the garlic, oregano, and beef broth. Return the browned beef to the pot. Add the mushrooms. Bring to a simmer. Reduce the heat to low, cover, and simmer for 2 to 2 ½ hours or until the beef is tender and starting to fall apart. (Stir once every 30 minutes.)

Gently remove the beef and set aside. Add the hot water to the sauce in the pot and bring to a gentle boil over medium heat. Stir in the noodles. Reduce heat to medium-low and cook, covered, at a slow simmer for 10 to 14 minutes or until the noodles are tender. Keep a close eye on the noodles and stir regularly to keep them from sticking to the bottom of the pan. (You may need to add a little water if there's not enough liquid.) When the noodles are tender but not mushy, remove the pot from the heat and return the beef to the pot.

Before serving, garnish with chopped parsley. (This is optional, but it definitely adds a bit of freshness to the dish.)

*Create lasting memories for those you love with old-fashioned comfort food. The meal, the company, the fragrance, and the love will leave fingerprints on their hearts that will never go away.*

# GRANDDADDY'S SPICY STEW MEAT

*I love trying new recipes, but it's the simple food of my childhood I enjoy the most. Mom never made anything too fancy. Food was easy to prepare, homemade, and comforting. And in many cases, it was food she grew up enjoying herself. These are the dishes that bring back memories.*

*Most of Mom's recipes were either from NaNa's recipe notebook or recipes she found and clipped from magazines. But this recipe came from my granddaddy. It's been one of my favorite dishes for as long as I can remember. Now that Granddaddy is gone, it has even more meaning. I think of him every time I make it, and I remember that he let me put lots and lots of bows on his head as I played "beauty parlor." That's a loving, and very patient, granddaddy!*

---

**MAKES 6 SERVINGS.**

Vegetable oil for browning meat

2 ½ pounds stew meat

All-purpose flour seasoned with salt and black pepper for dredging meat

1 yellow onion, chopped

1 (15-ounce) can tomato sauce

½ cup cider vinegar

½ cup sugar

1 teaspoon salt

½ teaspoon paprika

¼ teaspoon ground nutmeg

¼ teaspoon cayenne pepper (or more to taste)

1 heaping tablespoon all-purpose flour

1 cup water

6 cups hot, cooked rice for serving

Preheat the oven to 350 degrees.

Coat the bottom of a large, heavy skillet with vegetable oil and place over medium-high heat.

Dredge the pieces of meat in the seasoned flour and arrange in a single layer in the hot skillet without crowding. Brown the meat on all sides. Then remove to a roasting pan or Dutch oven and continue to brown the meat in batches.

After all the meat is brown and added to the roasting pan, add the onion to the skillet, turn the heat down to medium, and cook for 3 to 4 minutes, stirring occasionally.

Add the tomato sauce, vinegar, sugar, salt, paprika, nutmeg, and cayenne. Stir to scrape up the browned bits on the bottom of the skillet. Simmer for 15 minutes.

In a jar with a tight fitting lid, combine the flour and water. Shake to combine completely. Slowly pour the mixture into the simmering sauce, stirring constantly. Simmer for 3 minutes. Pour the contents of the pan over the meat in the roasting pan or Dutch oven. Stir and place in the preheated oven.

Bake for 2 hours, stirring once or twice during the baking time. Serve over hot, cooked rice.

NOTE: You can also make this in your slow cooker. Brown the meat and make the sauce as directed, but instead of placing the browned meat in a roasting pan, place it in the slow cooker. Then pour the sauce over the meat in the slow cooker and cook on low for 7 to 8 hours.

# SUNDAY PORK ROAST

*You don't have to make this only on Sundays. But a slow-cooking roast is the perfect Sunday supper. I absolutely love this roast. It is full of flavor and so tender it falls apart when you try to lift it from the pan. Oh . . . and the juices. Have mercy!*

**MAKES 8 SERVINGS.**

½ cup orange juice

½ cup red grapefruit juice

2 tablespoons firmly packed dark brown sugar

1 tablespoon honey

5 cloves garlic, minced

¼ cup chopped fresh parsley

2 teaspoons salt

1 teaspoon black pepper

2 teaspoons chili powder

1 teaspoon ground allspice

¼ teaspoon cayenne pepper

1 onion, chopped

4 bay leaves

1 (5-pound) Boston butt pork roast

Extra-virgin olive oil

In a medium bowl combine the orange juice, grapefruit juice, brown sugar, honey, garlic, parsley, salt, pepper, chili powder, allspice, and cayenne with a whisk. Stir in the onion. Add the bay leaves.

Place the roast in a shallow dish or in a large resealable plastic bag. Pour the marinade over the roast and marinate for 8 hours.

Preheat the oven to 275 degrees. Coat the bottom of a Dutch oven with olive oil and place over medium-high heat. Remove the roast from the marinade, reserving the marinade, and place in Dutch oven and brown on all sides. Place the marinade in a saucepan and bring to a boil. Simmer for 5 minutes. Pour the marinade over the roast. Cover and bake for 6 hours. Let stand for 20 minutes before serving.

# LOW AND SLOW PORK AND APPLES

*Pork, apples, and onions are a winning combination. Put them in a slow cooker and let them cook all day until they meld into something magical. You can prepare this dish the night before and put the slow cooker insert in the refrigerator. Put it back in the base and set it to low in the morning before you head out the door. You will come home to an absolutely amazing dinner. I like to serve this with potato and cheese pierogies purchased from the frozen food section of my grocery store. They cook very quickly so you can have a complete dinner on the table in about half an hour.*

**MAKES 6 TO 8 SERVINGS.**

1 large onion, cut in half and then thinly sliced

2 Granny Smith apples, peeled and sliced

1 (3-pound) pork sirloin roast

1 (32-ounce) package sauerkraut (in the deli section around prepared foods or the hot dogs)

2 cloves garlic, minced

½ cup brown sugar

½ teaspoon cayenne pepper

1 (12-ounce) container frozen apple juice concentrate, thawed

Arrange half of the onions and half of the apples in bottom of the slow cooker. Lay the roast on top of the onions and apples and arrange the remaining onions and apples on top of the roast. Rinse and drain the sauerkraut and spread over the top of the pork roast. Sprinkle with the minced garlic, brown sugar, and cayenne. Pour the juice over all. Cover and cook on low for 8 to 9 hours or until the pork begins to fall apart.

NOTE: For those of you who are suspicious of sauerkraut, fear not! Once it's rinsed and slow cooked, it tastes like really tender cabbage.

# PERFECT ROAST CHICKEN WITH POTATOES

*The perfect roast chicken is tender and juicy with crispy golden brown skin. The wondrous aroma that fills the house while it roasts is warm and inviting. It beckons anyone within sniffing distance to gather in the kitchen. A perfectly golden roast chicken can mend fences, break down barriers, butter up the in-laws, and stop siblings from fighting. Okay, maybe I'm reaching with that last one.*

*But seriously, considering the power of a roast chicken, it's surprising it isn't the centerpiece of family dinner at least once a week. The problem? Too many overcooked, dried-out failures.*

*I give you my word: this recipe will put an end to all that. This is my no-fail recipe for perfect roast chicken. The lemon, herbs, and onions delicately flavor the chicken while the chicken juices flavor the potatoes. The potatoes will be brown and crispy. The onions will caramelize. And by drying the skin before you cook it, you are guaranteed a crisp, golden skin.*

*Go ahead; break down some barriers.*

continued on next page

**MAKES 6 SERVINGS.**

4 large Yukon Gold potatoes, cut into quarters

2 red onions, cut into 8 wedges

1 (5-pound) roasting chicken

1 head garlic, cut in half crosswise to expose garlic

1 lemon, cut into four wedges

3 sprigs fresh thyme

2 sprigs fresh rosemary

1 ½ teaspoons sea salt

1 ½ teaspoons black pepper

Additional lemon, thyme, and rosemary for garnish, if desired

Preheat the oven to 425 degrees.

Arrange the potatoes and onions around the edge of a large roasting pan, with a few pieces in the center to create a "rack" for the chicken.

Rinse the chicken inside and out. Pat the outside of the chicken with paper towels, getting it as dry as possible. Place the chicken in the roasting pan on top of the potatoes and onions. Insert the garlic, lemon, thyme, and rosemary inside the chicken cavity. Tie the legs together with kitchen twine (to ensure even cooking). Sprinkle salt and pepper over the chicken and vegetables.

Roast the chicken for 30 minutes. Then cut a piece of foil just large enough to cover the top of the chicken. Lay the foil over the chicken and continue to roast for 30 minutes. Remove the foil and roast for another 30 minutes. Remove from the oven and let sit for 20 minutes before carving.

Garnish with lemon, thyme, and rosemary.

# CRISPY SOUTHERN FRIED CHICKEN

*There are a few tricks to flavorful, moist, and crispy fried chicken. The extra steps add a bit of time but you don't want to skip them. Soaking overnight in flavored buttermilk makes the chicken moist and infuses it with flavor. Adding cornstarch to the flour, and allowing the floured chicken to dry, makes the chicken extra crispy.*

*For a truly Southern Sunday supper, serve with Cheese Overload Macaroni and Cheese (page 168), greens cooked in bacon grease, and biscuits (page 39). Don't count the calories. Just invite your friends, enjoy the meal, and take a long walk after dinner. About 100 miles should do it.*

**MAKES 6 TO 8 SERVINGS.**

4 chicken legs

4 chicken thighs

Salt and pepper for seasoning chicken

5 cups buttermilk

3 teaspoons salt, divided

3 teaspoons black pepper, divided

3 teaspoons cayenne pepper, divided (feel free to add more if you like your chicken extra-spicy)

2 cups all-purpose flour

3 tablespoons cornstarch

1 teaspoon garlic powder

1 teaspoon Old Bay seasoning

1 teaspoon paprika

1 teaspoon onion powder

Peanut oil for frying

Pat the chicken with paper towels to dry. Sprinkle with salt and pepper and place in a dish deep enough to hold chicken and buttermilk.

In a large bowl whisk together the buttermilk, 2 teaspoons of the salt, 2 teaspoons of the pepper, and 2 teaspoons of the cayenne. Pour the buttermilk mixture over the chicken. Cover and place in the refrigerator overnight. If the chicken is not completely submerged in the buttermilk you will need to turn the chicken at least once.

Remove the chicken from the refrigerator 2 ½ hours before you are ready to fry.

Combine the flour, cornstarch, garlic powder, Old Bay, paprika, onion powder, and remaining 1 teaspoon of salt, pepper, and cayenne in a paper bag or in a shallow dish.

Place a cooling rack over a baking sheet.

Lift 1 piece of chicken out of the buttermilk and let the excess buttermilk drip off. Transfer to the flour mixture to coat completely, and then place on the rack. Repeat until all the chicken has been coated.

Place the rack in the refrigerator, uncovered, for 2 hours. (It's okay if it sits longer.) Remove from the refrigerator 15 to 20 minutes before frying.

Preheat the oven to 250 degrees.

Place a clean cooling rack over a baking dish and place it on the counter next to where you will fry the chicken.

*continued on next page*

Fill a deep, heavy skillet with peanut oil, high enough to come halfway up the chicken when frying. Heat over medium-high heat until the oil is 350 degrees. (If you don't have a thermometer, take a pinch of flour and drop it into the oil. If it starts to sizzle and bubble around the edges, your oil is hot enough.)

Use tongs to carefully arrange the chicken pieces skin side down in the hot oil. Don't crowd them. You want space in between the pieces. You will probably need to fry in two batches.

Fry for 8 minutes or until the chicken skin is deep golden. Turn the pieces over and fry another 7 or 8 minutes or until deep golden brown. If the chicken browns too quickly, turn the heat down. (If it browns too fast the inside won't have time to cook.)

Remove the chicken from the skillet and place it on the rack over the baking sheet. Place in the oven to keep warm while you fry the rest of the chicken.

NOTE: I love to make a chicken biscuit with leftover chicken and buttermilk biscuits. Simply remove the chicken from the bone, place on a hot split biscuit, and drizzle with honey. I know you're drooling!

# CRUNCHY HERBED CHICKEN

*Using stuffing mix as the coating for this chicken makes a flavorful and crunchy crust. Serve it with cranberry sauce and it's a little bit of Thanksgiving anytime of the year . . . without dirtying every single dish in the kitchen!*

**MAKES 4 TO 6 SERVINGS.**

1 cup sour cream

Juice of 1 lemon

½ teaspoon salt

½ teaspoon black pepper

½ teaspoon paprika

3 cloves garlic, minced

3 boneless, skinless chicken breasts, cut in half and lightly pounded

2 ½ cups herb-seasoned stuffing mix, coarsely crushed

¼ cup chopped parsley

¼ cup (½ stick) butter, melted

In a small bowl combine the sour cream, lemon juice, salt, pepper, paprika, and garlic. Place the chicken in a resealable plastic bag and pour the sour cream mixture over the chicken. Seal and then manipulate with your hands to make sure each piece is coated with the sauce. Lay flat in the refrigerator overnight.

The next night preheat the oven to 300 degrees. Spray a 9 x 13-inch casserole dish with nonstick cooking spray.

In a separate shallow dish combine the crushed stuffing mix and the parsley. Remove the chicken from the bag and completely coat each piece with the crushed stuffing. Place the pieces in the casserole dish, making sure they do not touch, and drizzle with the melted butter.

Bake for 45 to 50 minutes.

Remove from the oven and let sit for 10 minutes before serving.

*How wonderful it is that nobody need wait a single moment before starting to improve the world.*

—ANNE FRANK

# CHICKEN MARSALA

*Please don't assume this dish is too complicated to attempt at home. It's actually pretty simple to make. If you can brown cutlets and simmer a sauce, you can make delicious, restaurant-quality chicken Marsala in about thirty minutes.*

**MAKES 4 SERVINGS.**

½ cup all-purpose flour

½ teaspoon salt

¼ teaspoon black pepper

4 boneless, skinless chicken breasts, cut in half and pounded to ¼ inch thick

3 tablespoons extra-virgin olive oil, divided

5 tablespoons butter, divided

3 cloves garlic, minced

1 large shallot, finely chopped

2 ½ cups assorted sliced fresh mushrooms

¾ cup Marsala wine

1 cup chicken stock

1 teaspoon fresh rosemary leaves, plus additional sprigs for garnish

Salt and black pepper to taste

In a shallow dish combine the flour, salt, and pepper. Dust the chicken cutlets with the flour mixture, shaking off any excess.

Pour 1 tablespoon of the olive oil into a large, heavy skillet and place over medium heat. Add 1 tablespoon of the butter. When the butter is melted, arrange half of the cutlets in the skillet and cook for 2 to 3 minutes per side or until golden brown. Transfer to a plate and tent with foil to keep warm while you cook the remaining cutlets. Add another tablespoon of oil and another tablespoon of butter and cook the remaining cutlets, removing to the plate with the other cutlets once they are golden brown.

Add the remaining tablespoon of oil and 1 tablespoon of the butter to the skillet. As soon as the butter has melted, add the garlic and shallot and sauté for 1 minute, being careful not to let the garlic brown. Add the mushrooms and cook, stirring frequently, until the mushrooms have given off their liquid and have started to turn brown around the edges.

Add the Marsala and scrape the bottom of the pan to pick up any browned bits. Simmer until the wine is reduced by half. Add the stock and the rosemary leaves and simmer for 3 minutes. Stir in the remaining 2 tablespoons butter, stirring until melted.

Return the cutlets to the skillet, along with any accumulated juices, and turn to coat with the sauce. Gently simmer for 2 to 3 minutes to heat the cutlets through. Transfer the cutlets to a serving platter and spoon the sauce over the top. Garnish with rosemary springs.

> *What you leave behind is not engraved in stone monuments, but what is woven into the lives of others.*
>
> —UNKNOWN

# PISTACHIO-CRUSTED SALMON WITH CREAMY DIJON SAUCE

*This recipe is simple, flexible, and delicious! It is easy to make during the week and fancy enough to serve to company. You can substitute any nut for the pistachios, and you can substitute another firm fish for the salmon.*

**MAKES 4 SERVINGS.**

4 (6-ounce) salmon filets
Salt and black pepper
4 tablespoons Dijon mustard
4 tablespoons butter, melted
3 tablespoons honey
½ cup panko bread crumbs
½ cup finely chopped pistachios
¼ cup chopped parsley
1 lemon
Creamy Dijon Sauce (recipe follows)

Preheat the oven to 350 degrees. Spray a 9 x 13-inch casserole dish with nonstick cooking spray.

Remove the skin from the salmon and pat with paper towels to dry the fillets completely. Lightly salt and pepper the fillets. In a small bowl combine the Dijon, butter, and honey. In a shallow dish combine the bread crumbs, pistachios, and parsley.

Brush the Dijon mixture onto the salmon and then roll in the bread crumb mixture to coat. Place in the casserole dish. Squeeze the juice of half a lemon over the salmon. (Reserve the other half for garnishing.)

Bake for 20–22 minutes or until the salmon flakes easily with a fork.

Make the Creamy Dijon Sauce while the salmon is baking. To serve, spoon a small pool of sauce onto a plate and place a salmon fillet on top. Drizzle a little more sauce over the salmon. Garnish with a slice of the remaining lemon. You can also garnish with a sprig of parsley and a few pistachio nuts.

## CREAMY DIJON SAUCE

1 cup heavy cream
½ cup Dijon mustard
1 tablespoon butter, softened
Salt and black pepper to taste

Combine the heavy cream and Dijon mustard in a saucepan and bring to a low simmer over medium heat. Simmer for 5 minutes, whisking frequently. Whisk in the butter until melted. Remove from the heat and season with salt and pepper to taste.

# TEQUILA SHRIMP SKEWERS

*These are amazing cooked outside on a grill. Serve them with a pasta salad and fresh fruit for a light, refreshing, and colorful summer cookout menu. Since kids love food on sticks, I skewer cubes of chicken and vegetables and cook them beside the shrimp. You can also arrange assorted fresh fruit on skewers and stand them in a halved cantaloupe, pineapple, or other sturdy fruit. Food on a stick is just plain fun!*

NOTE: If using wooden skewers, soak them in water for 30 minutes before grilling.

**MAKES 4 TO 6 SERVINGS.**

1 cup vegetable oil

½ cup lime juice

Zest of 1 lime

¼ cup tequila

½ teaspoon salt

¼ teaspoon black pepper

¼ cup chopped fresh parsley

¼ cup chopped fresh cilantro, optional

3 pounds jumbo shrimp

1 large white onion

2 zucchinis

1 red, yellow, or orange bell pepper

3 limes, thinly sliced

10 tablespoons butter

In a medium bowl combine the oil, lime juice, zest, tequila, salt, pepper, parsley, and cilantro. Pour half of the marinade into a resealable bag. Reserve the other half. Clean, peel, and devein the shrimp, leaving the tails on. Place the shrimp in the bag, seal, and refrigerate 30 to 60 minutes, no longer.

Cut the onion, zucchinis, and pepper into large chunks. Remove the shrimp from the marinade and discard the marinade. Preheat your grill. While the grill is heating, alternately thread the shrimp, onion, zucchini, pepper, and lime on skewers.

Bring the reserved marinade to a boil in a small saucepan over medium-high heat. Reduce heat to medium-low and simmer until the marinade is reduced by half. Cut the butter into pieces and add to the marinade, stirring until melted. Set aside and keep warm.

Grill the skewers for approximately 2 to 3 minutes per side or until the shrimp is pink and opaque.

To serve, arrange the skewers on a serving platter and drizzle with the sauce.

# SEA BASS WITH BERRY-MANGO SALSA

*This is just plain gorgeous! Salsa is very versatile, and this berry version is no exception. In addition to spooning it over fish, you can spoon it over grilled chicken or scallops, serve it as an appetizer with pita chips, or spoon it over field greens for a colorful salad.*

**MAKES 4 SERVINGS.**

4 (6-ounce) Chilean sea bass fillets

Salt and black pepper

2 tablespoons extra-virgin olive oil

2 tablespoons butter

Berry-Mango Salsa (recipe follows)

Rinse and pat the fillets dry with a paper towel. Sprinkle with salt and pepper. Add the olive oil and butter to a heavy skillet and place over medium-high heat. Once the butter has melted and the pan is very hot, arrange the fillets in the pan and cook for 5 minutes or until golden brown on the bottom. Carefully turn the fillets over to brown for 4 to 5 minutes on the other side. The fish is done when it's opaque in the center. Remove from the pan and serve topped with salsa.

**BERRY-MANGO SALSA**

½ red bell pepper, seeded and finely chopped

½ red onion, finely chopped

1 jalapeño pepper, seeded and finely chopped

1 mango, peeled and chopped

1 ½ cups fresh mixed berries

Juice of 1 lime

1 teaspoon freshly grated ginger

⅓ cup chopped fresh cilantro

In a medium bowl combine the red pepper, onion, jalapeño, mango, berries, lime juice, ginger, and cilantro. Cover and chill for at least 1 hour.

# PAN-SEARED SCALLOPS ON A BED OF SPINACH WITH ORANGE BUTTER SAUCE

*The secret to pan-searing scallops is to make sure you dry them with paper towels before placing them in the hot pan. If you follow the simple instructions below, your scallops will look prettier and taste better than scallops served in most restaurants.*

**MAKES 4 SERVINGS.**

10 tablespoons butter, divided
12 ounces baby spinach leaves
2 shallots, finely chopped
2 cloves garlic, minced
⅓ cup white wine or chicken stock
⅓ cup heavy cream
3 ounces cream cheese, softened
½ teaspoon salt
½ teaspoon black pepper
Pinch of ground nutmeg
Pinch of cayenne pepper
¼ cup grated Parmesan cheese
16 large sea scallops
2 tablespoons extra-virgin olive oil
4 tablespoons orange marmalade

Place 2 tablespoons of the butter in a large, heavy skillet over medium heat. When the butter has melted and the pan is hot, place half of the spinach in the skillet, stirring to toss with the butter. Cook, stirring frequently, for 3 minutes or until just wilted. Remove to a colander to drain. Add the remaining spinach to the pan and cook in the same way, removing to drain after 3 minutes.

*continued on next page*

Remove any liquid from the pan and then melt another 2 tablespoons of the butter over medium heat. Add the shallots and garlic and sauté for 2 minutes, stirring constantly. Add the wine or chicken stock and simmer for 2 to 3 minutes or until reduced by half. Add the cream and cream cheese, stirring until the cream cheese is melted. Add salt, pepper, nutmeg, cayenne, and Parmesan cheese. Stir to combine.

Squeeze the liquid from the spinach and then add spinach to the sauce, turning to coat. Remove pan from heat.

Rinse the scallops and drain on paper towels. Place two layers of paper towels on top of the scallops and press gently to absorb any moisture. Place a cast-iron or other heavy skillet over medium-high heat and add the olive oil. As soon as the pan is very hot and the oil looks as if it's moving, arrange the scallops in a single layer, making sure they don't touch. (If they won't all fit in the pan, sear the scallops in two batches.) Once you have placed the scallops in the pan, do not touch them. After 1 minute, add 2 tablespoons of the butter to the pan. After another minute, gently lift one of the scallops to see if it is deep golden brown underneath. If not, cook an additional minute. Turn the scallops over and cook for 2 minutes on the other side. Remove the scallops from the pan.

In a small saucepan, melt the remaining 4 tablespoons of butter with the marmalade, stirring to combine.

To serve, transfer the creamed spinach to a serving platter. Arrange the seared scallops over the spinach. Drizzle the scallops with the marmalade butter. Serve immediately.

> *Do your little bit of good where you are; it's those little bits of good put together that overwhelm the world.*
>
> —DESMOND TUTU

# LEMON HERB-CRUSTED FISH FILLETS

*I try to eat fish a couple of times a week. This is one of my favorite ways to prepare almost any fish fillet. For a quick weeknight dinner, serve it with a green veggie or on a bed of baby greens with a light vinaigrette dressing.*

**MAKES 4 SERVINGS.**

4 skinless firm white fish fillets (sea bass, halibut, cod)

Salt and black pepper

3 tablespoons extra-virgin olive oil

6 tablespoons fresh lemon juice, divided

½ cup Italian-style bread crumbs

½ cup grated Parmesan cheese

¼ cup chopped parsley

4 tablespoons butter, melted

1 teaspoon lemon zest

Preheat the oven to 350 degrees. Spray a baking pan with nonstick cooking spray.

Pat fillets with paper towels to dry. Sprinkle with salt and pepper.

In a small bowl combine the olive oil with 3 tablespoons of the lemon juice and brush on the fillets. In a shallow dish combine the bread crumbs, Parmesan cheese, and parsley. Coat the fillets with the bread crumb mixture and place in the baking pan.

Bake for 20 minutes or until the fish flakes easily with a fork.

Move the oven rack to the top position and turn on the broiler. Broil the top of the fillets for 1 minute or until brown and crispy.

In a small bowl combine the melted butter, remaining 3 tablespoons lemon juice, and the lemon zest. Arrange the fillets on a serving dish and drizzle with the lemon butter.

# HOT CHICKEN SALAD CASSEROLE

*Every Southern gal has a version of this recipe—one that's been passed down from their mama or granny. You will find it on the buffet table at every church social, potluck, or funeral. (Yes, we bring food to funerals.) If something ails ya or there's been a death in the family, you can be sure a hot chicken salad casserole is headed your way. A well-prepared Southerner always has one of these casseroles in her freezer, ready to go.*

**MAKES 8 SERVINGS.**

7 tablespoons butter, divided

1 ½ cups sliced fresh mushrooms

1 (10.5-ounce) can cream of mushroom soup

½ cup mayonnaise

½ cup sour cream

1 whole 2 ½ to 3-pound chicken, cooked, skinned, and cut into bite-size pieces

3 stalks celery, chopped

1 onion, chopped

1 can sliced water chestnuts, drained

½ cup sliced almonds

2 cups shredded Swiss cheese

1 cup Italian-style bread crumbs

1 tablespoon dried chopped parsley

Preheat the oven to 350 degrees. Spray a 9 x 13-inch casserole dish with nonstick cooking spray.

Melt 3 tablespoons of the butter in a skillet over medium heat. Add the mushrooms and sauté until they release their liquid, stirring occasionally until the liquid evaporates. Set aside to cool.

In a small bowl combine the cream of mushroom soup, mayonnaise, and sour cream. In a large bowl combine the chicken, celery, onion, water chestnuts, and the sautéed mushrooms. Stir in the soup mixture. Spoon into the casserole dish.

Sprinkle an even layer of almonds over the casserole, followed by the Swiss cheese. Melt the remaining 4 tablespoons of butter in a small microwavable bowl and add the bread crumbs and parsley. Sprinkle over the cheese.

Bake for 40 to 50 minutes or until the casserole is bubbly and golden brown.

NOTE: Cranberry sauce is the perfect accompaniment with this casserole.

# CHICKEN AND RICE CASSEROLE

*This type of casserole is great for bringing to potlucks or to a family going through a difficult time. It's also a great casserole to keep in your family dinner rotation. You can make the casserole in advance and bake it when ready to serve. The kids probably won't even notice the spinach!*

**MAKES 8 SERVINGS.**

½ cup (1 stick) butter, divided

1 medium onion, finely chopped

2 stalks celery with leaves, chopped

4 ounces sliced fresh baby bella mushrooms

2 cloves garlic, minced

¼ cup dry sherry

4 ounces cream cheese

1 (10-ounce) box frozen spinach, thawed and squeezed dry

3 cups cooked chicken

2 ½ cups shredded sharp Cheddar cheese, divided

1 (6-ounce) package long-grain and wild rice mix, prepared as directed

1 (10.5-ounce) can cream of mushroom soup

1 cup sour cream

½ cup milk

½ teaspoon salt

½ teaspoon black pepper

½ cup sliced almonds

1 cup Italian-style bread crumbs

½ cup grated Parmesan cheese

Preheat the oven to 350 degrees. Spray a 9 x 13-inch casserole dish with nonstick cooking spray.

Melt ¼ cup of the butter in a large skillet over medium heat. Add the onion, celery, and mushrooms and sauté for 5 minutes or until onions are transparent. Add the garlic and sherry and sauté for 5 additional minutes. Remove from the heat and stir in the cream cheese to melt. Add the spinach once the cream cheese has melted.

In a large bowl combine the chicken, 1 ½ cups of the Cheddar cheese, the prepared rice, cream of mushroom soup, sour cream, milk, salt, and pepper. Stir in the onion mixture and combine.

Spoon the mixture into the pan. Sprinkle the remaining 1 cup Cheddar cheese over the top. Top with sliced almonds.

Melt the remaining ¼ cup of the butter in a small microwavable bowl and stir in the bread crumbs and Parmesan cheese to combine. Spread evenly over the top of the casserole.

Bake for 35 to 40 minutes or until hot and bubbly and the top is golden brown.

# WHOLE WHEAT BAKED PENNE WITH VEGETABLES

*If you find comfort in baked pasta dishes with lots of rich flavors and gooey cheese—and who doesn't?—here's an option that is a little healthier. It's not necessarily low in calories, and I wouldn't call it health food, but it is a healthier option.*

*The sauce starts with ground turkey breast instead of beef or pork, so it already has less fat than a typical baked pasta dish. I also use canned tomato sauce instead of a jar of marinara sauce so it doesn't have the added sugar typically found in a jarred sauce. Whole wheat pasta and the addition of veggies kicks up the nutritional value so, all in all, this version isn't too bad. Okay . . . there is cheese. But I love cheese so very, very much.*

**MAKES 6 TO 8 SERVINGS.**

1 pound ground turkey breast

1 (8-ounce) package sliced fresh baby bella mushrooms

2 zucchinis, cut in half and sliced

2 to 3 cloves garlic, minced

3 (8-ounce) cans no-salt-added tomato sauce

1 teaspoon dried basil

½ teaspoon dried oregano

Dash ground cinnamon

¼ teaspoon sea salt

¼ teaspoon ground black pepper

1 pound box whole wheat penne, cooked 1 minute less than directed on box and drained

4 cups baby spinach leaves

½ cup grated Parmesan cheese

2 cups shredded Italian cheese blend

3 or 4 fresh basil leaves, torn, for garnish

Preheat the oven to 350 degrees and spray a 2-quart casserole dish with nonstick cooking spray.

In a Dutch oven over medium-high heat, break up and cook the ground turkey until no longer pink. Add the mushrooms, zucchini, and garlic and continue to cook for 2 to 3 minutes. Add the tomato sauce, basil, oregano, cinnamon, salt, and pepper and bring to a gentle boil. Reduce the heat and simmer for 10 minutes. Add the cooked penne and the spinach and stir to combine.

Spoon half of the pasta mixture into the casserole dish. Sprinkle with half of the Parmesan cheese and half of the shredded Italian cheese blend. Cover with the remaining pasta mixture, remaining Parmesan cheese, and remaining Italian cheese.

Bake for 30 minutes or until the cheese is melted and beginning to brown. Remove from the oven and let sit for 10 minutes. Go ahead. Sneak some of the crispy cheesy edges. You know you want to. Before serving, garnish with torn basil leaves. (They'll hide the missing edges so no one will be the wiser.)

# EASY CHICKEN ENCHILADAS

*If you want an easy recipe for chicken enchiladas that will impress, this is it. No one will believe you didn't bring home Mexican food from a restaurant.*

**MAKES 6 TO 8 SERVINGS.**

1 (14-ounce) can mild enchilada sauce
Plain rotisserie chicken from the deli section of your grocery store
2 cups sour cream, plus extra for serving
1 package low-sodium taco seasoning mix
1 can green chilies, drained (mild, medium, or hot)
Jalapeño peppers, seeded and finely chopped, optional
1 (16-ounce) can traditional refried beans
10 to 12 (8-inch) flour tortillas
1 package Mexican rice mix, prepared as directed on the package
2 cups shredded Mexican cheese blend
2 green onions, sliced
Lettuce, shredded for garnish
Tomato, chopped for garnish
Guacamole, optional
Salsa, optional

Preheat the oven to 350 degrees. Spray a 9 x 13-inch casserole dish with nonstick cooking spray. Spoon a little of the enchilada sauce into the bottom of the dish—just enough to coat.

Remove the skin from the chicken and shred the meat into bite-size pieces. In a large bowl mix 2 cups of sour cream, taco seasoning mix, and chilies. (If you like more kick, add the jalapeños.) Stir in the chicken.

Spoon about 2 tablespoons of the refried beans down

*continued on next page*

the center of a tortilla. Top with a few spoonsful of the chicken mixture and a few spoonsful of the prepared rice. Roll up the tortilla and place seam side down in the prepared dish.

Pour the remaining enchilada sauce down the center of the enchiladas and top with the cheese. Sprinkle with the green onions.

Bake for 30 to 45 minutes or until the cheese has melted and the enchiladas are heated through.

To serve, garnish with lettuce and tomatoes, and serve with sour cream, guacamole and salsa if desired.

> *Kind words can be short and easy to speak, but their echoes are truly endless.*
>
> —MOTHER TERESA

# FIESTA NOODLE BAKE

*This recipe started out as a simple beef and noodle casserole I was making for a very busy friend and her family. It was kind of bland, so I kept playing with the flavors until I got it right. The addition of chili powder and cream cheese turned an ordinary casserole into something special. Pray about someone you can make it for. There's always someone who would be blessed to receive a warm, cheesy casserole.*

**MAKES 6 TO 8 SERVINGS.**

1 ½ pounds ground beef

2 cloves garlic, minced

1 small green bell pepper, finely chopped

½ teaspoon salt

½ teaspoon black pepper

1 (15-ounce) can tomato sauce

1 teaspoon sugar

Dash of ground cinnamon

2 teaspoons chili powder (or more to taste)

¼ teaspoon crushed red pepper flakes (or more to taste)

¼ teaspoon dried thyme leaves

1 (11-ounce) package wide egg noodles

1 (8-ounce) package cream cheese, softened

1 cup sour cream

1 (10-ounce) box spinach, thawed and squeezed dry

6 green onions, sliced

2 cups shredded Cheddar cheese

Brown the ground beef in a large skillet over medium-high heat, breaking up the meat as it browns. After it is cooked through, drain the fat and then add the garlic, green pepper, salt, and pepper to the skillet. Cook for about 3 minutes and then stir in the tomato sauce, sugar, cinnamon, chili powder, red pepper flakes, and thyme. Bring to a boil, reduce the heat to medium-low, and simmer for 30 minutes.

While the sauce is simmering, cook the noodles 1 minute less than directed on the package and then drain.

Preheat the oven to 350 degrees. Spray a 2-quart shallow casserole dish with nonstick cooking spray.

In a large bowl combine the cream cheese, sour cream, spinach, and green onions. Add the warm, drained noodles to the mixture and stir to coat the noodles completely. Add the sauce to the noodle mixture and stir to combine. Transfer to the casserole dish. Cover with the shredded Cheddar cheese and bake for 30 minutes or until hot and bubbly and the cheese has melted.

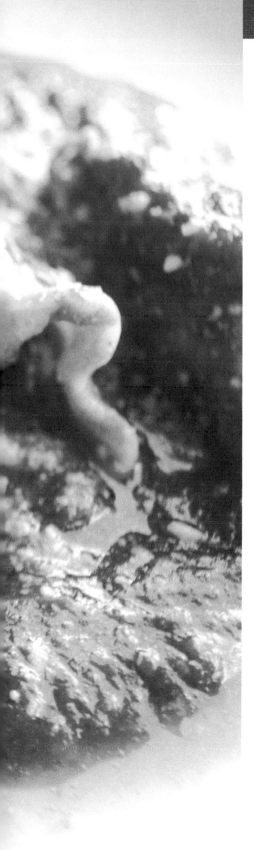

# LASAGNA PINWHEELS

*Just about everyone loves lasagna . . . don't they? Well, it's always been one of my favorites, and I've noticed that when I go out to an Italian restaurant, my dinner companions seem to choose lasagna from the menu more than any other dish. Lasagna is comfort food in my book. Let's be honest. Anything with noodles and cheese is a comfort food.*

*Lasagna is a great dish to make ahead when you are expecting dinner guests, but it's almost become too ordinary since it's often the go-to dish to serve guests. I wanted to do something a little unexpected while still keeping the traditional flavors of lasagna, so I came up with a new twist. I combined my love for lasagna with my love for pretty, swirly things and came up with Lasagna Pinwheels. Now I can serve a favorite meal but in a new way.*

*I love using chicken in my marinara sauce, so my version is made with chicken. But you can change this up by using Italian sausage, ground beef, short ribs, pork, ground turkey, or veggies.*

*Wait till you see the delighted reactions of your guests when they see your unexpected, and quite spectacular, presentation. They will think you worked much harder than you really did. The truth is, this takes less time to make than traditional lasagna. But I won't tell.*

---

**MAKES 8 SERVINGS.**

1 tablespoon extra-virgin olive oil

1 tablespoon butter

1 pound boneless, skinless chicken, cut into bite-size pieces

1 yellow onion, finely chopped

3 cloves garlic, minced

2 (28-ounce) cans crushed tomatoes

2 teaspoons dried basil

1 teaspoon dried oregano

Dash of ground cinnamon

*continued on next page*

Pinch of crushed red pepper flakes

Salt and black pepper to taste

1 (16-ounce) box lasagna noodles

1 (15-ounce) container low-fat ricotta cheese

1 (10-ounce) box frozen chopped spinach, thawed and squeezed dry

½ cup grated Parmesan cheese

Dash of ground nutmeg

1 large egg

3 cups shredded mozzarella cheese, divided

¼ teaspoon salt

¼ teaspoon black pepper

Add the olive oil and butter to a large, heavy skillet and place over medium heat. When the butter has melted, increase the heat to medium-high. When the skillet is hot, add the chicken and cook until the chicken is browned on all sides. Add the onion and garlic and continue to cook for 1 minute. Add the tomatoes, basil, oregano, cinnamon, red pepper flakes, and salt and pepper to taste. Reduce the heat to low and simmer for 30 minutes.

While the sauce is simmering, boil the noodles 1 minute less than directed on the package. Drain, rinse with cool water to stop the cooking process, and lay each noodle flat on a towel to dry.

In a medium bowl combine the ricotta cheese, spinach, Parmesan cheese, nutmeg, egg, 1 cup of the shredded mozzarella, salt, and pepper.

Preheat the oven to 350 degrees. Spray a 9 x 13-inch casserole dish with nonstick cooking spray. Spoon enough of the sauce into the casserole dish to cover the bottom.

Lay a noodle in front of you and spread a heaping ⅓ cup of the ricotta cheese mixture over the noodle (as if you are icing it). Beginning with one end, roll the noodle into a spiral. Place the spiral, seam side down, in the casserole dish. Continue with the remaining noodles and filling. Spoon the remaining sauce over and around the noodles. (If making the day ahead of serving, stop at this point and cover with foil and store in the refrigerator.)

Sprinkle the remaining 2 cups of shredded mozzarella over the pinwheels. Bake for 30 to 40 minutes or until hot and bubbly and the cheese has melted and begins to turn golden around the edges.

# SHRIMP SCAMPI

*Butter, garlic, and lemon. What's not to love?! And, extra bonus . . . it comes together as quickly as you can cook the pasta! LOVE!*

**MAKES 6 SERVINGS.**

½ pound linguine

6 tablespoons butter

1 tablespoon extra-virgin olive oil

1 shallot, finely chopped

5 garlic cloves, minced

2 pounds large shrimp, washed, peeled, and deveined

½ teaspoon salt

½ teaspoon black pepper

½ cup dry white wine

½ cup fresh-squeezed lemon juice

Pinch of crushed red pepper flakes (or more to taste)

⅓ cup chopped fresh Italian flat-leaf parsley

½ cup grated Parmesan cheese

Bring large pot of water to a boil. As the water is heating, gather all the ingredients so the dish can come together in the ten minutes or so it will take the pasta to cook. When the water has come to a boil, add the pasta and cook for 1 minute less than directed on the package. Drain.

In a large skillet melt the butter over medium heat. Add the olive oil, shallots, and garlic and sauté for 3 minutes, stirring every 20 to 30 seconds. Add the shrimp to the pan and sprinkle with the salt and pepper. Continue to sauté for 3 minutes, turning so the shrimp turns pink on both sides. Add the wine, lemon juice, and red pepper flakes. Simmer for 2 minutes or until the shrimp is opaque.

Return cooked pasta to the pot, and pour the shrimp and juices over the cooked linguine and toss to combine.

Transfer to a shallow serving dish and top with parsley and grated Parmesan cheese. Serve immediately.

# SAUSAGE AND PEPPER LINGUINE

*This recipe came to me in a dream, which happens to me from time to time. Perhaps it happens when I go to bed hungry. Or maybe I just have food on my mind all the time.*

*I dreamed a friend was standing over my shoulder in my kitchen, guiding me as I was cooking. When I woke up I realized he was giving me ingredients my Nanny used often, and it sounded delicious. I had just moved, so I quickly unpacked my kitchen, found my pots and pans, and whipped this up. It was delicious! And my new kitchen smelled just like Nanny's! Ahhhh . . . home.*

**MAKES 8 SERVINGS.**

1 tablespoon extra-virgin olive oil

2 pounds Italian sausage links cut into diagonal slices (8 to 10 links) (use sweet, mild, hot, or a combination)

1 onion, peeled and cut in half, then cut into thin half circles

1 green bell pepper, seeded and cut into strips

1 red bell pepper, seeded and cut into strips

1 yellow bell pepper, seeded and cut into strips

1 orange bell pepper, seeded and cut into strips

3 cloves garlic, minced

1 pound sliced fresh mushrooms

¼ teaspoon (or to taste) crushed red pepper flakes

1 (28-ounce) can crushed tomatoes

2 teaspoons dried basil leaves

½ teaspoon dried oregano leaves

Dash of ground cinnamon

1 pound linguine

1 head escarole, roughly chopped

Grated Parmesan cheese for serving

Fresh basil for garnish, optional

Place a large, heavy skillet over medium to medium-high heat and coat with olive oil. When the pan is hot, add a layer of sausage slices but do not crowd the pan. When the sausage slices are brown and crispy on one side, turn them over and brown the other side. (You do not have to cook them through. Just brown them.) Remove the browned sausage slices to a large, heavy pot and then brown the next batch. Repeat until all of the sausage slices are browned.

Add the onions to the drippings in the pan and stir to coat. As soon as they are soft, add the peppers, garlic, mushrooms, and red pepper flakes. Sauté for 3 minutes, stirring often, and then add to the pot with the sausage slices.

Remove the skillet from the heat and place the pot over the heat. Add the crushed tomatoes, basil, oregano, and cinnamon and stir to combine. Bring just to a boil over medium-high heat, and then reduce heat to low, cover, and simmer for 30 minutes, stirring occasionally.

After about 15 minutes, boil the pasta as directed on the box. Two minutes before it is done, add the escarole. Continue to boil for 1 minute and then drain. (This will be 1 minute short of the recommended cooking time on the box.)

Add the drained pasta and escarole mixture to the pot and stir to coat with the sauce. Remove from the heat and cover. Let it sit for 5 to 10 minutes so the pasta will absorb some of the sauce and cook completely.

Serve with Parmesan cheese and garnish with fresh basil if desired. Now your house smells like my Nanny's house too.

# PASTA IN CREAMY SAVORY PUMPKIN SAUCE

*My sweet friend Ian tests just about every dish I make. And while he never complains, there is definitely a look he's not good at disguising when he isn't exactly thrilled about a recipe I'm working on. When I described this recipe, he wrinkled his nose and with more than a hint of skepticism said, "You're gonna do what?!" After his second helping and a request to take the rest home, he promised never to doubt me again. That promise lasted about two weeks. That's when I told him there was sauerkraut in the Low and Slow Pork and Apples (page 112). Let's not tell him about the rutabaga in the Chicken and Harvest Vegetable Soup (page 79). We'll just keep that between us.*

**MAKES 6 TO 8 SERVINGS.**

1-pound box gemelli, bowties, or other small pasta

1 (5-ounce) package baby spinach leaves

4 tablespoons butter

1 onion, chopped

1 red bell pepper, chopped

3 cloves garlic, minced

½ pound cooked and crumbled mild sausage

1 cup chicken broth

4 ounces cream cheese, softened

1 (15-ounce) can solid pumpkin

1 cup heavy cream

1 cup grated Parmesan cheese, plus more for serving

½ teaspoon ground sage

½ teaspoon salt

½ teaspoon black pepper

Pinch of ground nutmeg

Pinch of cayenne pepper

Fresh sage leaves for garnish, if desired

*continued on next page*

Cook the pasta 1 minute less than directed on the package, adding the spinach to the boiling water about 1 minute before the pasta is done. Drain and return the pasta and spinach to the pot but do not put the pot back on the heat.

While the pasta is cooking, melt the butter in a large skillet over medium heat. Add the onion, red pepper, and garlic and sauté for 3 minutes. Stir in the sausage and cook for another minute. Add the chicken broth and bring to a simmer.

In a medium bowl combine the cream cheese, pumpkin, and cream until smooth. Stir in 1 cup of the Parmesan cheese, sage, salt, pepper, nutmeg, and cayenne. Stir into the sausage mixture.

Pour the sauce over the pasta and stir to combine. Transfer to a serving dish and top with additional Parmesan cheese and, if desired, sage leaves.

# LINGUINE WITH CLAM SAUCE

*The garlicky wine sauce is so delicious you won't want to leave a single drop, so make sure you serve this with crusty bread to sop it all up.*

**MAKES 8 SERVINGS.**

1 pound linguine

2 tablespoons salt

½ cup (1 stick) butter

1 onion, chopped

2 cups sliced fresh mushrooms

4 cloves garlic, minced

⅓ cup chopped fresh Italian flat-leaf parsley, plus more for serving

½ teaspoon dried oregano leaves

½ teaspoon black pepper

½ cup dry white wine

2 cups chopped canned clams with juice

1 cup grated Parmesan cheese, plus more for serving

Bring a large pot of water to a boil, and add the pasta and salt. Cook for 1 minute less than directed on the package. Drain. (If you begin the sauce as soon as you drop the pasta into the boiling water, the pasta and the sauce will be done at the same time.)

Melt the butter in a large skillet over medium heat. Add the onion, mushrooms, and garlic and sauté for 3 minutes. Stir in the parsley, oregano, pepper, wine, and clams. Simmer for 5 minutes. Add the cooked linguine and stir to coat. Add 1 cup grated Parmesan cheese and toss to coat the pasta.

Turn the pasta out into a large, shallow serving bowl and sprinkle with additional Parmesan cheese and parsley. Serve immediately.

# BAKED TORTELLINI

*This is a basic recipe you can easily modify. You can add grilled chicken, browned ground beef or sausage, mushrooms, onions, peppers, and any other veggies that you like. It comes together quickly so it's a great go-to when someone needs a meal delivered.*

**MAKES 6 TO 8 SERVINGS.**

1 (20-ounce) package cheese tortellini

⅔ cup mascarpone cheese, softened

1 (26-ounce) jar marinara sauce

½ cup grated Parmesan cheese, plus extra for serving

Dash of ground cinnamon

1 ½ cups fresh baby spinach leaves

2 cups Italian cheese blend

Preheat the oven to 350 degrees. Spray a 2-quart casserole dish with nonstick cooking spray.

Bring a large pot of water to a boil. Add the tortellini and boil for 2 to 3 minutes. Drain.

In the warm pot you boiled the tortellini in, but off the heat, whisk together the mascarpone cheese, marinara sauce, Parmesan cheese, and cinnamon. Stir in the spinach leaves. Add the drained tortellini and stir to combine. Transfer to the casserole dish and top with the Italian cheese blend.

Cover and bake for 20 minutes. Uncover and bake an additional 20 minutes or until the cheese is melted and the casserole is hot and bubbly.

Garnish with extra grated Parmesan cheese if desired. (When is extra cheese not a good idea?)

# POBLANO POPPER STUFFED PORTOBELLOS

*A very filling and flavorful vegetarian dish. It's pretty rich, so if you are serving as a side dish, serve it with something light, like grilled chicken or fish. If serving as the entrée, serve with a simple green salad with vinaigrette.*

**MAKES 4 SERVINGS AS AN ENTRÉE OR 8 AS A SIDE DISH.**

4 poblano peppers

8 portobello mushrooms, stemmed

4 tablespoons extra-virgin olive oil

1 teaspoon salt

½ teaspoon ground black pepper

6 tablespoons butter, divided

1 small onion, finely chopped

1 jalapeño pepper, seeded and finely chopped

½ teaspoon ground cumin

8 ounces cream cheese, softened

1 (10-ounce) box frozen chopped spinach, thawed and squeezed dry

1 cup cooked white or brown rice

½ cup sour cream

1 ½ cups shredded sharp Cheddar cheese, divided

1 ½ cups shredded Monterey Jack cheese, divided

3 tablespoons chopped fresh cilantro

1 cup panko bread crumbs

½ cup grated Parmesan cheese

Preheat the broiler. Line a baking pan with foil and place the poblanos on the pan. Place the pan 6 inches under the broiler and broil, turning until blackened on all sides. This should take about 5 minutes. Once blackened, place in a plastic bag until cool to the touch. Remove the peppers from the bag and use a paper towel to wipe away the blackened skin. Cut the peppers in half and scrape out the seeds. Finely chop the peppers and set aside.

Remove the mushroom gills by scraping them out with a spoon. Lightly brush both sides with the olive oil and sprinkle with salt and pepper. Place under the broiler for 8 to 12 minutes or until soft, turning over after 4 minutes. Line a plate with paper towels. Place the cooked mushrooms hollow side down on the lined plate to allow the liquid to drain.

Melt 4 tablespoons of the butter in a large skillet over medium heat. Add the onion and sauté for 2 minutes. Add jalapeños and sauté for an additional 2 minutes. Add the cumin and cream cheese, stirring until the cream cheese has melted. Then add spinach to the pan along with the rice, sour cream, and chopped poblanos. Stir to combine. Remove from the heat and transfer to a bowl. Mix in 1 cup of the Cheddar and 1 cup of the Monterey Jack and the cilantro.

Move the oven rack to the center position and preheat the oven to 325 degrees.

Divide the filling mixture among the mushroom caps, mounding slightly, and place in a large casserole dish. Top the filling with the remaining ½ cup of Cheddar and Monterey Jack cheeses.

In a small microwavable bowl melt the remaining 2 tablespoons of butter and stir in the panko and Parmesan cheese. Sprinkle on top of cheeses.

Bake for 25 minutes or until the cheeses have melted and the bread crumbs are golden brown.

# ROASTED VEGGIE FLATBREAD PIZZA

*I could eat this every single day. I've listed my favorite toppings, but you can make this with a variety of toppings, sauces, and cheeses. My son prefers his like a traditional pepperoni pizza. Barbecue sauce, grilled chicken, red onions, cilantro, and Cheddar is another yummy combination. If you are cooking for kids, let each child make his or her own individual-size pizza. Set up a toppings bar and give everyone a ball of dough and let the fun begin. It's a great way to get kids interested in cooking.*

**MAKES TWO 9-INCH RECTANGLES.**

½ of a red bell pepper, cut into thin slices

1 cup sliced fresh mushrooms

½ of a small red onion, sliced

2 tablespoons extra-virgin olive oil

1 store-bought pizza dough (found in the deli section of your grocery store)

⅔ cup prepared pesto sauce

3 cups shredded cheese (mozzarella and Provolone)

2 small Roma tomatoes, thinly sliced

Preheat the oven to 425 degrees.

Arrange the red peppers, mushrooms, and onions on a cookie sheet and drizzle with olive oil. Roast for 20 to 25 minutes or until the edges begin to brown. Remove and increase the oven temperature to 450 degrees.

Divide dough in half and press each half into ¼-inch thin rectangles on cookie sheets. Spread each with half of the pesto and top each with half of the shredded cheeses. Arrange the roasted vegetables and tomato slices on top of the cheese.

Bake for 12 to 15 minutes or until the cheese has melted and the crust is crisp and brown around the edges.

# VEGETABLES AND SIDES

*You don't choose your family. They are God's gift to you, as you are to them.*
—DESMOND TUTU

Side dishes fill the empty space on your dinner plate, complement the entrée, and round out the meal to make it complete, just as friends and family do in life. For years my life was pretty lonely—definitely not complete.

Between the loss of my husband and living on the opposite coast from most of my family, our home felt quiet and lonely. Empty chairs around the dinner table, fewer stockings hung on the mantel at Christmas, and having to sing "happy birthday" to Nick by myself made me keenly aware of the smallness of my family of two. But letting people in is not easy for me. Loss and betrayal have resulted in protective walls around my heart. Big ones. Walls to keep me from being hurt again. (Sound familiar?)

For years, I was so afraid of letting anyone in I found myself completely alone with my sweet little boy, who didn't understand why our home wasn't filled with family on special occasions and why there were so many empty chairs at our dinner table. I knew I desired our home to be filled with people, laughter, and memories, but I wasn't sure how to make that happen. But God did.

Over the years, God put little cracks in my walls. He led us to a sweet little church where we were immediately embraced as family, and He brought a handful of treasured friends to fill the empty chairs around our table and the voids in our lives.

Friends who filled in the gaps when I was unable to pick Nick up from school.

Friends who let me be "Aunt LeLe" to their children.

Friends who continue to eat my kitchen experiments no matter how many times I set off the smoke alarm.

I may not have the life I imagined, but it is my life and I am grateful for the blessings of family and friends who love Nick and me and fill in some of the empty spaces in our hearts, and the empty chairs around our dinner table. Life now is definitely complete.

Savory Bread Pudding

Twice-Baked Potato Casserole

Sweet Oven-Roasted Corn on the Cob

Brown Rice Pilaf

Roasted Veggies

Maple-Glazed Winter Squash

Cheesy Au Gratin Potatoes

Cheesy Corn Pudding

Creamed Corn

Parmesan-Crusted Potatoes

Spaghetti Squash with Orange Butter

Cheese Overload Macaroni and Cheese

Spinach Gratin

Cauliflower Soufflé

Roasted Sweet Potatoes with Spicy Glaze

Mushroom Gratin

Creamy Cheddar Grits

Apple-Cranberry Chutney

Roasted Brussels Sprouts with Pancetta

Sautéed Spinach and Sugar Snap Peas

Roasted Potatoes with Bacon and Cheese

Green Bean Bundles

Creamy Broccoli-Cauliflower Casserole

# SAVORY BREAD PUDDING

*The main differences between a savory bread pudding and stuffing is the addition of eggs and cream. The final result, though, is a flavorful and moist stuffing that works great as a side dish any time of the year. I have also served this as part of my Thanksgiving menu, and it made everyone thankful.*

**MAKES 8 SERVINGS.**

5 cups 1-inch bread cubes from a rustic loaf of bread

3 tablespoons butter

3 leeks, white part only, cut in half lengthwise and sliced

2 cups sliced fresh mushrooms (any variety or mixed)

4 cloves garlic, minced

¼ cup chopped flat-leaf parsley

1 (10-ounce) box frozen chopped spinach, thawed and squeezed dry

½ teaspoon salt

½ teaspoon black pepper

1 cup browned and drained Italian sausage (or 2 ounces cooked diced pancetta or 1 cup cooked bacon)

½ cup chicken stock

5 large eggs

2 cups heavy cream

2 teaspoons Worcestershire sauce

1 ½ cups grated Parmesan cheese, divided

Preheat the oven to 350 degrees. Butter or spray a 2-quart casserole dish with nonstick cooking spray.

Place the bread on a cookie sheet and bake for 15 minutes.

Melt the butter in a large skillet over medium heat. Add the leeks, mushrooms, and garlic and sauté for 5 minutes. Add the parsley, spinach, salt, and pepper and stir to combine. Add the cooked sausage and chicken stock. Set the pan aside to cool.

In a medium bowl combine eggs, cream, Worcestershire, and ½ cup of the Parmesan cheese.

Place the toasted bread and the cooled mushroom mixture in a large bowl. Pour the egg mixture into the bowl and stir to combine. Set aside for 10 minutes to allow the bread cubes to soak.

Pour the mixture into the casserole dish and top with the remaining 1 cup Parmesan cheese. Bake uncovered for 1 hour. Remove from the oven and let sit for 15 minutes before serving.

# TWICE-BAKED POTATO CASSEROLE

*Buttery, creamy, cheesy mashed potatoes . . . with bacon! I'm giving you a heads-up—be prepared for someone to lick the serving dish. I'm not kidding! It happens. They are that good.*

**MAKES 8 SERVINGS.**

8 russet or Yukon Gold potatoes
3 teaspoons salt, divided
¼ cup (½ stick) butter, softened
½ cup heavy cream
1 cup sour cream
4 ounces cream cheese, softened
3 green onions, chopped
½ teaspoon black pepper
3 cups shredded Cheddar cheese, divided
6 strips cooked bacon

Peel the potatoes and cut into quarters. Place in a large pot and cover with water. Add 2 teaspoons of the salt. Bring to a boil over high heat. Reduce the heat to medium-high and simmer for 20 to 30 minutes or until the potatoes are tender. Drain and return to the pot.

Preheat the oven to 350 degrees. Spray a 2-quart casserole dish with nonstick cooking spray.

While the oven is preheating, add the butter, cream, sour cream, cream cheese, green onions, remaining 1 teaspoon salt, pepper, and 1 cup of the Cheddar cheese to the drained potatoes. Mash until smooth. Transfer to the baking dish and top with the remaining 2 cups of cheese. Crumble the bacon and sprinkle over the top.

Bake for 30 minutes or until the cheese is melted and the potatoes are bubbly.

# SWEET OVEN-ROASTED CORN ON THE COB

*I can't pass up a big ol' bin of corn on the cob at my local farmers' market. Fresh, in-season corn is delicious and crispy and sweet and . . . well . . . it's perfect! Roasting is my favorite way to prepare corn on the cob when I'm making it for a crowd. You can prepare it in advance, which I love, and you can make it just about any flavor you like so it will go with any menu. Throw something on the grill and throw these in the oven.*

**PER EAR OF CORN**

1 tablespoon butter
1 tablespoon honey
Salt and black pepper to taste

Preheat the oven to 400 degrees. Line a rimmed cookie sheet (large enough to hold the number of ears of corn you are roasting) with foil. Trust me . . . you do not want to skip this step. If the honey mixture leaks out, it will burn onto the cookie sheet.

Remove the husk and silk from each ear of corn. Cut a piece of foil about 9 inches in length.

In a small microwavable bowl melt the butter. Stir in the honey and salt and pepper. Spoon half of the butter mixture onto the center of the piece of foil and spread it into a line about the length of the ear of corn. Lay the corn on the mixture. Spoon the remaining honey butter on top of the corn. Roll around to coat. Wrap the foil up and around the corn and seal. Place on the cookie sheet and roast for 20 minutes.

You can serve the ears in the foil or unwrap them and pile them on a serving dish and top with a pat of butter and a drizzle of honey. Not because it's needed. Just because it looks pretty!

NOTE: You can replace the honey with Parmesan cheese and/or you can add any herbs or spices.

# BROWN RICE PILAF

*I could eat this rice every day! It's flavorful and colorful and the perfect side for just about any entrée. However, this doesn't need to be a side dish. Just spoon it into a bowl and grab your fork.*

**MAKES 6 SERVINGS.**

1 tablespoon extra-virgin olive oil

1 shallot, finely chopped

1 to 2 cloves garlic, minced

1 ½ cups whole grain brown rice

3 ¼ cups low-sodium chicken or vegetable broth

1 large carrot, peeled and shredded

3 green onions, chopped

½ cup dried cranberries

½ cup chopped walnuts, toasted

Zest of an orange

Black pepper to taste

⅓ cup chopped fresh Italian flat-leaf parsley

Place a saucepan over medium-high heat. Add the olive oil and shallots. Cook, stirring frequently, until the shallots are soft. Add the garlic and brown rice. Cook and stir for 1 minute. Add the broth and carrots. Bring to a boil, reduce the heat, cover, and simmer for 30 minutes.

Remove from the heat and fluff with a fork. Stir in the green onions, cranberries, walnuts, orange zest, pepper, and parsley, and serve.

> *All great change in America begins at the dinner table.*
>
> **—RONALD REAGAN**

# ROASTED VEGGIES

*Roasting brings out the sweetness in vegetables and creates a depth of flavor you don't get using other cooking methods. When you roast veggies, the edges caramelize and they look beautifully rustic. Introduce your kids to a variety of vegetables by serving them roasted. They just might fall in love with them!*

Vegetables (refer to list on opposite page)

Extra-virgin olive oil

Kosher or sea salt

Fresh ground black pepper

Minced garlic

Herbs or spices of choice, optional (rosemary, thyme, and cardamom work really well)

Melted butter, optional

Preheat the oven to 425 degrees. Clean, trim, cut, and place the vegetables in a medium bowl. Drizzle with olive oil (just enough to coat very lightly) and then sprinkle with salt, pepper, garlic, and herbs, if using. Toss to evenly coat, and transfer to a shallow baking pan or a jelly-roll pan. Roast until crispy around the edges and tender on the inside. Place in a serving dish and drizzle with a little melted butter, if desired.

## ROASTING GUIDE

Asparagus spears (12 minutes)

Baby carrots (15 minutes)

Bell peppers, quartered and seeded (12 minutes)

Haricots verts or other green beans (15 minutes)

Leeks, halved lengthwise and cut into 2-inch slices (15 minutes)

Mushrooms (15 minutes)

New potatoes, cut in half (30 to 40 minutes)

Sweet potatoes or root vegetables, cut into 2-inch chunks (30 to 40 minutes)

Yellow squash or zucchini, cut into 2-inch slices (10 minutes)

I also love to mix up a variety of veggies and roast them together. Just make sure you cut the sturdier veggies (like potatoes) into smaller chunks than your softer veggies (like zucchini or mushrooms) so they will be done at the same time.

# MAPLE-GLAZED WINTER SQUASH

*This maple glaze is perfect for fall and winter holidays because it's not as rich or heavy as most vegetable casseroles. The cardamom gives the squash a very unique flavor. A little goes a long way, so not much is needed. Please do not go out and buy the spice just to make this recipe. Cardamom is one of the more expensive spices. I am fortunate to have a natural food store that sells spices in bulk so I am able to purchase just a spoonful. If you do not have this option and don't want to spend the money on a jar of cardamom, combine equal parts cinnamon and ginger and use it as a replacement. It won't be exactly the same, but it's much easier on the wallet!*

**MAKES 8 SERVINGS.**

1 butternut or 2 acorn squash, peeled, seeded, and cut into 1-inch cubes

¼ cup (½ stick) butter, melted

¼ cup pure maple syrup

¼ cup firmly packed dark brown sugar

½ teaspoon salt

¼ teaspoon black pepper

¼ to ½ teaspoon ground cardamom (according to taste)

Preheat the oven to 400 degrees. Spray a 15 x 10-inch jelly-roll pan with nonstick cooking spray.

Place the squash chunks in a large bowl. In a medium bowl combine the butter, maple syrup, brown sugar, salt, pepper, and cardamom and pour over squash. Toss to coat. Transfer to the jelly-roll pan.

Roast for 40 to 45 minutes or until tender but crispy, stirring about halfway through.

# CHEESY AU GRATIN POTATOES

*Cheese makes everything better, doesn't it? Actually, cheese and butter. It makes sense that adding extra of both would result in the best au gratin potatoes. So that's what I did.*

*I played around with au gratin and scalloped potato recipes until I came up with one that always works for me. "Au gratin" and "scalloped" are often used interchangeably, but there is a difference. Scalloped potatoes are thinly sliced potatoes baked in a white sauce. Au gratin potatoes are baked with cheese! So, of course, I always make au gratin!*

*Here's a tried-and-true recipe. The trick is to parboil the potatoes before assembling the dish so the casserole cooks evenly and the topping doesn't burn before the potatoes are done.*

---

**MAKES 8 SERVINGS.**

4 pounds Yukon Gold potatoes

3 tablespoons salt, plus extra for seasoning

6 tablespoons grated Parmesan cheese

Black pepper

3 tablespoons butter, cut into small cubes

5 cups shredded Cheddar cheese (or use combination of your favorite melting cheeses)

2 cups heavy cream

1 cup milk

Paprika, optional

Peel and thinly slice the potatoes. (A mandolin will make an easy task of this.) Place the sliced potatoes in a large pot and cover with water. Add 3 tablespoons of salt to the water. Bring to a boil, reduce the heat, and simmer for 15 minutes. Remove the pan from the heat and carefully drain the potatoes. Set the potatoes aside until cool enough to handle.

Preheat the oven to 350 degrees. Spray a 9 x 13-inch casserole dish with nonstick cooking spray or rub with butter.

Layer a third of the potatoes in the bottom of the baking dish. Sprinkle with a third of the Parmesan cheese and some salt and pepper. Dot with 1 tablespoon of the butter. Sprinkle with 1 cup of the shredded Cheddar cheese. Repeat the layers two more times.

In a large measuring cup combine the cream and the milk. Slowly pour over the potatoes until you can just see the cream coming up on the sides. You may not need all of the liquid. Top with the remaining 2 cups Cheddar cheese and sprinkle with paprika.

At this point you can cover the casserole dish with foil and store in the refrigerator until ready to bake (up to two days).

When ready to bake, place the uncovered casserole dish on a jelly-roll pan and bake for 45 minutes or until the cheese is melted, the casserole is bubbly, and the potatoes are fork-tender. (If you made ahead and stored in the refrigerator, leave on the counter for 45 minutes before baking.)

Remove from the oven and let sit for 15 to 20 minutes to let the cheese set up and the sauce thicken.

# CHEESY CORN PUDDING

*I love cooking with corn. I especially enjoy recipes where corn is the star ingredient, like Creamed Corn (page 164) and this yummy Cheesy Corn Pudding. This is an awesome side dish for grilled meat, poultry, or seafood, and it's even pretty yummy on your holiday table. Now, I will warn you . . . this is not figure friendly. It's one of those dishes I put in the category of "only when having company." That means I make it for a group of people and, if there are any leftovers, I send the rest home with my guests. That way I get my taste and then say bye-bye to the temptation.*

**MAKES 6 TO 8 SERVINGS.**

1 (15-ounce) can whole kernel corn, drained

1 (15-ounce) can creamed corn

1 cup sour cream

½ cup (1 stick) butter, melted

Dash of cayenne pepper

¼ teaspoon kosher salt

¼ teaspoon ground black pepper

1 (8-ounce) package corn muffin mix

1 ½ cups shredded sharp Cheddar cheese

Preheat the oven to 350 degrees. Spray a 2-quart casserole dish with nonstick cooking spray.

In a large bowl combine both cans of corn, sour cream, butter, cayenne, salt, and pepper. Once combined, stir in the muffin mix. Spoon into the casserole dish and bake for 40 to 45 minutes or until golden brown. Top with the shredded cheese and bake an additional 20 minutes or until the cheese has melted and the center is set.

# CREAMED CORN

*I have a problem. It's detrimental to my health and my waistline, but I just can't help it. I love cream cheese. There . . . I've said it! Admitting you have a problem is the first step to recovery.*

*I always keep a block or two (or three or four) of the creamy goodness in my refrigerator so I can melt a few spoonsful into recipes in need of a little something extra. Like creamed corn! Cream cheese isn't a typical ingredient in creamed corn, but adding it took my recipe over the top. The first time I tried it I ate the entire batch! I just couldn't stop myself.*

**MAKES 6 SERVINGS.**

5 slices bacon, cut into ½-inch pieces

2 small or 1 large shallot, chopped

1 (1-pound) bag frozen corn, thawed (I like to use the white and yellow mix), or 3 cups fresh corn if it's in season

¼ teaspoon black pepper

Dash of cayenne pepper

⅓ cup water

3 ounces cream cheese, softened

2 teaspoons snipped fresh chives

Fry the bacon in a deep skillet over medium-high heat. Drain on paper towels.

Remove all but 2 tablespoons of the bacon grease from the skillet. Add the shallots and cook, stirring frequently, for 1 minute or until the shallots just begins to brown. Reduce the heat to medium and add the corn, pepper, cayenne, and water. Bring to a simmer. Cover and cook for 4 minutes or until the corn is heated through and tender. Add the cream cheese in small pieces and stir to melt.

To serve, transfer to a serving dish and sprinkle with crispy bacon pieces and chives.

Now take a bite.

Drooling is unattractive.

Grab a napkin.

# PARMESAN-CRUSTED POTATOES

*The Parmesan cheese forms a flavorful crust as these potatoes roast in the oven. Easy and delicious!*

½ cup (1 stick) butter, cut into slices

⅔ cup grated Parmesan cheese

8 medium red potatoes, cut in half lengthwise

Arrange the butter slices in the bottom of a 9 x 13-inch baking pan. Place the pan in a cold oven and preheat the oven to 400 degrees. Remove the pan as soon as the butter has melted and continue to preheat the oven.

Sprinkle the Parmesan cheese evenly over the melted butter. Arrange the halved potatoes, cut side down, over the cheese.

Bake for 40 to 45 minutes or until the potatoes are tender and the cut side is crispy.

> *The generous will themselves be blessed, for they share their food with the poor.*
>
> —PROVERBS 22:9

# SPAGHETTI SQUASH WITH ORANGE BUTTER

*I love the color, texture, and crunchiness of spaghetti squash, and this is my favorite way to serve it. It's even fancy enough for holidays and special occasions. And the orange butter is yummy on biscuits too!*

**MAKES 6 SERVINGS.**

½ cup chopped pecans
1 (3 to 4 pounds) spaghetti squash
½ cup (1 stick) butter, softened
Zest of 2 oranges
2 tablespoons freshly squeezed orange juice
1 tablespoon dark brown sugar
¼ teaspoon ground nutmeg
Dash or two of ground cloves
½ teaspoon salt

Preheat oven to 350 degrees. Place pecans in a single layer on an ungreased cookie sheet and bake in preheated oven for 8 minutes. Remove and set aside to cool.

Pierce the squash several times with a fork. Place in a glass casserole dish and microwave, uncovered, on high heat for 10 to 12 minutes or until it starts to give when you poke at it. Remove from the microwave. Cut in half lengthwise and scrape out the seeds. Using a fork, scrape the squash "strands" from their shells into a large bowl.

In a small bowl cream together the butter, orange zest, orange juice, brown sugar, nutmeg, cloves, and salt.

Stir the orange butter into the squash, and transfer to a serving bowl. Top with the toasted pecans.

# CHEESE OVERLOAD MACARONI AND CHEESE

*I think I have finally come up with the best mac and cheese ever! I took every macaroni and cheese recipe I had ever clipped and laid them out in front of me in my pursuit of the best-ever mac and cheese. I then looked at each one and determined what I liked best and what I knew I wouldn't like. I combined my favorite elements of each recipe and then . . . just because it seemed like the right thing to do . . . I added MORE CHEESE!*

*Y'all, there are six cheeses in my mac and cheese! That's right . . . SIX! I was up to five, which was fairly impressive. Then, right before I started mixing my cooked pasta with the sauce ingredients, I reached for the cream cheese sitting on the top shelf of my refrigerator. It called out to me and, well . . . I just had to do it.*

*The first velvety bite rocked my world. In fact, just thinking about it makes my eyes tear up. The memory of the cheesy goodness combined with the crunchy, buttery bread crumb topping simply makes my eyes roll back in my head. Seriously . . . give me a moment to reminisce.*

*This is one of those recipes you want to serve to company, bring to a potluck, or take to a family that is in the midst of a crisis. Do not, I repeat, do not keep this in your house. Indulge once, and then send it on its merry way!*

---

**MAKES 8 SERVINGS.**

1 pound pasta (elbow, spirals, etc.)

¼ cup all-purpose flour

2 heaping teaspoons dry mustard

1 teaspoon kosher or sea salt

½ teaspoon black pepper

A few dashes of ground nutmeg

A few dashes to ⅛ teaspoon cayenne pepper (depending on your taste)

¾ cup melted butter, divided

5 large eggs, beaten

2 cups half-and-half

1 cup heavy cream

1 ¾ cups grated Parmesan cheese, divided

3 cups shredded sharp Cheddar, divided

Preheat the oven to 350 degrees. Spray a deep 9 x 13-inch casserole dish with nonstick cooking spray.

Cook the pasta 1 minute less than directed on the package. As it cooks, combine the flour, dry mustard, salt, pepper, nutmeg, and cayenne in a small bowl. Use a whisk to blend and then whisk in ½ cup of the melted butter until there are no lumps.

In a large bowl combine the beaten eggs, half-and-half, and heavy cream. Whisk the flour mixture into the egg mixture until combined.

Stir in 1 cup of the Parmesan cheese, 2 cups of the sharp Cheddar, 2 cups of the Monterey Jack, and the Swiss.

After you have drained the pasta, place the 2 tablespoons softened butter and the cream cheese in the hot pot (off of the heat) so it begins to melt. Once it begins to melt, add the drained (but still hot) pasta to the pot and stir to coat the pasta with the butter and cream cheese. (Please pause just to gaze upon the creaminess!)

Once the pasta is coated, add the egg and flour mixture

3 cups shredded Monterey Jack, divided

1 cup shredded Swiss

2 tablespoons butter, softened

4 ounces cream cheese, cut into cubes, softened

¾ cup Italian-style panko bread crumbs

*When making this recipe I didn't skimp on the cream, butter, or cheese. I poured it on with abandon. This is how we are to love each other . . . lavishly and with abandon, and without measuring the risk.*

and stir to combine. Pour the entire mixture into the casserole dish and then top with the remaining 1 cup of Cheddar and Monterey Jack cheeses.

In a small bowl combine the bread crumbs with the remaining ¾ cup Parmesan cheese. Stir in the remaining ¼ cup of the melted butter. Sprinkle the mixture evenly over the top of the mac and cheese.

Bake for 45 minutes or until bubbly and beginning to brown.

Turn your broiler on and broil for ONLY 1 to 2 minutes. Keep a close eye on this. You want the top to be lightly golden brown and crunchy . . . not burned. It will happen very quickly, so stand right beside your oven and watch it closely.

Remove from the oven and let sit for 15 minutes.

Take a spoon and pull the cheesy gooey goodness from the casserole dish. Stare at it. Grab your pepper mill and grind some black pepper over the top. Stare at it some more. Choke back the tears as you take your first bite. Say thank You to God for the many varieties of cheese. Now run a few laps to save yourself from any lasting effects of said cheesy gooey goodness. Do not wallow in guilt. Just enjoy and then move on. Tomorrow is another day, and steamed broccoli will be there. Hmm . . . you know, broccoli is really good with a little cheese on top.

# SPINACH GRATIN

*I use a lot of spinach. I add it to so many things—soups, casseroles, pasta dishes, stir-frys . . . When mixed into another recipe, you can't really taste the spinach, so it's a great way to get extra nutrients into your kids without them noticing.*

*There are times I don't want to be sneaky with spinach. Sometimes I want it to be the star of the dish. On those occasions, I either sauté spinach with a little bit of shallots for flavor, or, if I'm planning a fancy meal, I make Spinach Gratin. It's not likely you will have leftovers, but if you do, add some roasted chicken and you have another amazing meal.*

**MAKES 8 SERVINGS.**

½ cup (1 stick) butter

1 large shallot, finely chopped

2 cloves garlic, minced

¼ cup all-purpose flour

2 cups heavy cream, divided

1 cup chicken or vegetable stock

4 ounces cream cheese, softened

¼ teaspoon ground nutmeg

1 teaspoon salt

½ teaspoon black pepper

⅛ teaspoon cayenne pepper

1 ½ cups grated Parmesan cheese

5 (10-ounce) boxes frozen chopped spinach, thawed and squeezed dry

2 cups shredded Gruyere or Swiss cheese

½ cup Italian-style bread crumbs

Preheat the oven to 400 degrees. Spray a 9 x 13-inch casserole dish with nonstick cooking spray.

In a large, deep skillet melt the butter over medium heat. Add the shallots and sauté until they are soft and translucent, about 10 minutes. Add the garlic and sauté for 1 minute. Sprinkle with the flour and cook, stirring constantly, for 1 minute to cook off the flour taste.

Slowly add 1 cup of the cream, whisking to keep the flour from clumping. Once the mixture is smooth, whisk in the remaining cream and the stock. Cut the cream cheese into pieces and add it, stirring until melted. Stir in the nutmeg, salt, pepper, and cayenne and simmer for 3 minutes.

Add the Parmesan cheese to the sauce. Stir in the spinach. Transfer the mixture to the casserole dish and top with the shredded Gruyere. Sprinkle with the bread crumbs.

Bake for 30 minutes or until hot and bubbly and the topping is golden brown.

# CAULIFLOWER SOUFFLÉ

*Don't let the word* soufflé *prevent you from making this dish. I promise it's not difficult to make and won't collapse if you bump the oven. I just call it a soufflé because the beaten egg whites make it light and puffy.*

**MAKES 6 SERVINGS.**

1 head cauliflower

⅓ cup water

¼ cup plus 1 tablespoon butter, plus more to prepare the casserole dish

2 tablespoons all-purpose flour

1 cup heavy cream

½ teaspoon salt

½ teaspoon black pepper

1 tablespoon chopped chives

4 tablespoons Italian-style bread crumbs, divided

4 tablespoons grated Parmesan cheese, divided

3 large eggs, separated

1 cup shredded Swiss cheese

Preheat the oven to 400 degrees. Butter a 2-quart casserole dish.

Wash the cauliflower and cut the florets off of the stalk. Cut into large chunks and place in a microwave-safe dish. Add the water and cover the dish. Microwave on high for 5 minutes, stirring halfway through the cooking time. Drain.

Place ¼ cup of the butter in a large skillet over medium heat. When the butter has melted and the skillet is hot, sprinkle the flour over the butter and whisk until smooth. Whisk in the heavy cream. Simmer for 3 minutes, stirring constantly. Stir in the salt, pepper, chives, 2 tablespoons of the Italian-style bread crumbs, and 2 tablespoons of the Parmesan cheese. Stir in the egg yolks and Swiss cheese, and remove from the heat. Stir the cauliflower into the sauce.

Place the egg whites in a clean, dry bowl and beat until stiff. Carefully fold the beaten whites into the cauliflower mixture, then spoon into the prepared casserole dish.

Melt the remaining 1 tablespoon butter in a microwave-safe small bowl. Stir in the remaining 2 tablespoons bread crumbs and the remaining 2 tablespoons Parmesan cheese. Sprinkle the mixture over the top of the cauliflower. Bake for 30 minutes, or until puffy and golden brown.

# ROASTED SWEET POTATOES WITH SPICY GLAZE

*A balanced combination of sweet and spicy adds just the right amount of zing to golden, caramelized roasted sweet potatoes. The rich color of the potatoes looks beautiful next to any entrée.*

**MAKES 6 TO 8 SERVINGS.**

3 pounds sweet potatoes, peeled and cut into large cubes

3 tablespoons vegetable oil

1 teaspoon salt

½ teaspoon black pepper

4 tablespoons butter

3 tablespoons pure maple syrup

1 teaspoon chili powder

⅛ teaspoon cayenne pepper

Preheat the oven to 450 degrees.

Place the sweet potato cubes in a large bowl, drizzle with oil, and sprinkle with salt and pepper. Toss to coat, and transfer to a 15 x 10-inch jelly-roll pan. Arrange in a single layer. Roast for 35 to 45 minutes or until potatoes are tender and golden brown around the edges. Remove from the oven.

While the potatoes are roasting, melt the butter in a small saucepan and stir in the maple syrup, chili powder, and cayenne pepper. Simmer for 2 minutes.

To serve, transfer the roasted sweet potatoes to a serving dish and drizzle with the maple butter glaze.

> *Great opportunities to help others seldom come, but small ones surround us every day.*
>
> **—SALLY KOCH**

# MUSHROOM GRATIN

*I love just about every variety of mushroom. I've combined three of my favorites in this recipe. The sauce has a wonderful flavor but still allows the earthiness of the mushrooms to come through.*

**MAKES 8 SERVINGS.**

½ cup plus 3 tablespoons butter, divided, plus more for preparing casserole dish

3 cloves garlic, minced

2 cups sliced baby bella mushrooms

1 cup sliced shiitake mushrooms

1 cup sliced oyster mushrooms

2 tablespoons all-purpose flour

2 teaspoons Dijon mustard

½ teaspoon crushed dried thyme

½ teaspoon chopped chives

2 tablespoons chopped fresh parsley

¼ teaspoon salt

¼ teaspoon ground black pepper

⅓ cup sherry or white wine

½ cup heavy cream

⅓ cup Italian-style bread crumbs

⅓ cup Parmesan cheese

Preheat the oven to 350 degrees. Butter a shallow 1-quart casserole dish.

Melt ¼ cup of the butter in a large skillet over medium heat. Add the garlic and mushrooms. Sauté until most of the liquid has evaporated. Spoon the mushrooms into a bowl and set aside. Add 3 tablespoons of the butter to the skillet to melt. Sprinkle with the flour and cook, stirring constantly, for 1 minute. Stir in the mustard, thyme, chives, parsley, salt, and pepper. Whisk in the sherry and heavy cream. Bring to a slow boil, reduce heat to medium-low, and simmer, stirring frequently, until the sauce has thickened.

Return the mushrooms to the skillet, being careful not to add any of the liquid that collected in the bowl. Stir to combine the mushrooms and sauce. Transfer to the casserole dish.

Melt the remaining ¼ cup of butter in a microwave-safe dish. Add the bread crumbs and Parmesan cheese to the melted butter and stir to moisten the crumbs. Sprinkle over the casserole. Bake for 20 to 25 minutes or until hot and bubbly and lightly browned.

# CREAMY CHEDDAR GRITS

*Grits are a Southern staple, mostly for breakfast but also with dinner or the traditional low-country shrimp and grits. If you order eggs, bacon, and toast for breakfast in the South, your plate will always arrive with a big spoonful of white grits. I'm certain admitting I don't really like the soupy pool of white stuff next to my eggs would have me branded a traitor and thrown out of the South. So I won't say that. But I can definitely get excited about the grits served with supper—the heartier stone-ground grits. Add cream and cheese and . . . boom yow! A delicious alternative to mashed potatoes or rice.*

**MAKES 8 SERVINGS.**

6 cups low-sodium chicken broth, divided

2 cups water

2 cups stone-ground grits

1 teaspoon salt

2 cups heavy cream

4 ounces cream cheese, softened

¼ cup (½ stick) butter, softened

¼ teaspoon black pepper

Dash or two of cayenne pepper

3 cups shredded Cheddar cheese

Heat 2 cups of the chicken broth in a saucepan over medium heat and keep warm.

In a separate large saucepan bring 4 cups of the chicken broth and the water to a boil over high heat. Whisk in the grits and salt. Reduce the heat to low so it's just simmering. Cover and simmer for 30 minutes, stirring occasionally. If the grits get too thick too quickly, add the warm chicken stock a half a cup at a time as needed.

Remove the lid and stir in the cream. Cover and continue to simmer on low heat for 30 minutes, or until the grits are cooked. Cut the cream cheese and butter into cubes and stir into the grits along with the pepper and cayenne. As soon as the butter and cream cheese have melted, remove the pan from the heat and stir in the shredded Cheddar cheese.

Serve hot.

# APPLE-CRANBERRY CHUTNEY

*Chutney adds great flavor and texture to roasts and grilled meats. It's a lower-calorie, lower-fat alternative to using rich, creamy sauces to flavor meats. This apple-cranberry combination is amazing with a simple pork roast. Use any leftovers as a condiment on sandwiches.*

**MAKES 2 CUPS.**

3 tablespoons butter

2 large sweet onions, chopped

¼ cup firmly packed brown sugar

2 Granny Smith apples, peeled and thinly sliced

1 cup fresh cranberries

½ teaspoon salt

¼ teaspoon black pepper

2 dashes ground cloves

2 dashes ground allspice

2 dashes ground ginger

⅓ cup apple juice, plus more if necessary

2 tablespoons cider vinegar

Add the butter to a large skillet and place the skillet over medium heat. When the butter has melted, add the onions and sauté for 5 minutes. Add the brown sugar and stir to coat the onions. Sauté for 5 more minutes. Add the apples, cranberries, salt, pepper, cloves, allspice, ginger, apple juice, and vinegar. Reduce the heat to low, and cook, stirring occasionally, for 1 ½ hours. If the pan becomes dry, add a little more juice. You don't want any liquid left in the pan, but you don't want it so dry it burns on the bottom.

*She opens her arms to the poor and extends her hands to the needy.*

**—PROVERBS 31:20**

# ROASTED BRUSSELS SPROUTS WITH PANCETTA

*Totally serious . . . these are the best Brussels sprouts I have ever had. This is my favorite way to make them. The only problem is there are never enough left to serve because I can't stop myself from eating them before my guests arrive. This recipe has turned Brussels sprouts haters into lovers!*

**MAKES 4 TO 6 SERVINGS.**

1 tablespoon olive oil
¼ pound pancetta, chopped
2 tablespoons butter
1 shallot, finely chopped
1 pound Brussels sprouts, trimmed and cut in half lengthwise
Black pepper

Preheat the oven to 425 degrees. Spray a 15 x 10-inch jelly-roll pan with nonstick cooking spray.

Coat the bottom of a large skillet with the olive oil and place over medium-high heat. Add pancetta to the pan and cook, stirring frequently, until crisp. Drain on paper towels, leaving any drippings in the skillet.

Add the butter and shallots to the skillet. Cook, stirring constantly, for 1 minute to begin to brown the shallots. Add the Brussels sprouts and stir to coat. Transfer to the jelly-roll pan and bake for 30 minutes. Remove from the oven and sprinkle with pepper to taste. Do not add salt!

To serve, place in a shallow serving bowl and top with pancetta. Taste at this point and add salt only if needed.

# SAUTÉED SPINACH AND SUGAR SNAP PEAS

*Cook this very quickly to keep the vibrant green color of the vegetables.*

**MAKES 4 TO 6 SERVINGS.**

1 pound sugar snap peas

2 tablespoons extra-virgin olive oil

2 tablespoons butter

1 teaspoon sesame oil

1 shallot, minced

3 cloves garlic, minced

1-inch piece ginger, minced

½ teaspoon salt

½ teaspoon black pepper

1 (6-ounce) bag baby spinach leaves, rinsed

⅓ cup white wine or chicken stock

Remove the strings from the sugar snap peas. Add the olive oil, butter, and sesame oil to a large skillet and place over medium-high heat. When the pan is hot, add the shallots and sauté for 2 minutes. Add the sugar snap peas, garlic, ginger, salt, and pepper. Continue to sauté, stirring frequently, for 3 minutes or until the sugar snaps are crisp-tender. Add the spinach and wine or stock and cook, stirring frequently, until the spinach has wilted.

# ROASTED POTATOES WITH BACON AND CHEESE

*Golden roasted potatoes with crispy bacon and gooey cheese, drizzled in bacon fat . . . um . . . yes, please!*

3 pounds medium Yukon Gold potatoes, quartered

1 tablespoon plus 1 teaspoon salt

8 slices bacon, cut into 1-inch pieces

2 tablespoons extra-virgin olive oil

3 cloves garlic, minced

½ teaspoon black pepper

¼ teaspoon paprika

1 ½ cups shredded Cheddar cheese

⅓ cup chopped fresh Italian flat-leaf parsley

Place the rack in the second from bottom position and preheat the oven to 425 degrees.

Place the potatoes in a large pot and cover with cold water. Add 1 tablespoon of the salt and bring to a boil over high heat. Reduce the heat and gently simmer for 10 minutes. Drain and arrange on paper towels to dry completely.

While the potatoes are cooling, cook the bacon in a skillet until crispy. Drain on paper towels. Reserve the grease in the skillet. Drizzle half of the reserved bacon grease over the bottom of a 15 x 10-inch jelly-roll pan.

Place the potatoes in a large bowl and toss with the olive oil, garlic, remaining 1 teaspoon salt, pepper, and paprika. Arrange the potatoes, cut sides down, on the jelly-roll pan.

Bake for 30 minutes. Remove from the oven and reduce the temperature to 350 degrees.

Turn the potatoes over and sprinkle with the Cheddar cheese and crispy bacon. Quickly reheat the remaining bacon grease and drizzle over the potatoes. Return the pan to the oven and bake for 15 to 20 minutes or until the cheese is melted. Remove to a serving platter and sprinkle with parsley.

Serve immediately.

# GREEN BEAN BUNDLES

*Serving individual portions in a special way doesn't really take much extra effort. You can serve pureed sweet potatoes or winter squash in a hollowed-out orange half, or rice pilaf on a portobello mushroom cap. Or bundle green beans and wrap them in bacon. Little "packages" make people feel special. Just knowing you spent a little extra time to make their plates beautiful lets them know you really care. It's a simple little thing, but the rewards are immeasurable.*

**MAKES 6 SERVINGS.**

2 pounds fresh green beans, ends trimmed
½ cup (1 stick) butter, melted
1 cup brown sugar
1 teaspoon chili powder
Dash or two of cayenne pepper
2 teaspoons Worcestershire sauce
1 clove garlic, minced
⅛ teaspoon black pepper
½ pound bacon, slices cut in half

Preheat the oven to 375 degrees.

Bring a large pot of water to a boil. Add the beans and boil for 2 minutes. Drain and rinse with very cold water until the beans are cool. Spread the beans on a clean towel or paper towels to dry.

In a medium bowl combine the butter, brown sugar, chili powder, cayenne, Worcestershire, garlic, and black pepper.

Divide the beans into bundles with 7 beans in each. Wrap each bundle with half a slice of bacon and place the bundle seam side down in a 9 x 13-inch baking dish. Spoon 1 tablespoon of the brown sugar mixture into the center of each bundle, on the bacon.

Bake for 30 minutes or until the bacon is crispy. Serve hot.

# CREAMY BROCCOLI-CAULIFLOWER CASSEROLE

*When I'm asked to bring a vegetable dish to a potluck, this is the one most requested. One taste and you'll know why. It's rich and creamy so it works best with grilled chicken or fish, or as part of a holiday menu.*

**MAKES 8 SERVINGS.**

2 cups broccoli crowns, very coarsely chopped

3 cups cauliflower florets, very coarsely chopped

½ cup (1 stick) butter

2 cloves garlic, minced

⅓ cup finely chopped onion

½ teaspoon salt

½ teaspoon black pepper

3 tablespoons all-purpose flour

1 cup milk

⅓ cup white wine or chicken stock

4 ounces cream cheese, softened

1 (10-ounce) box frozen chopped spinach, thawed and squeezed dry

1 ½ cups grated Parmesan cheese, divided

Preheat the oven to 350 degrees. Spray a 9 x 13-inch casserole dish with nonstick cooking spray.

Partially cook the broccoli and cauliflower, either by steaming in a pot on the stovetop or in the microwave for approximately two to three minutes. The vegetables should be firm. Immediately pour the steamed vegetables into a colander and rinse with cold water to stop the cooking process. Set aside to drain.

In a heavy skillet melt the butter over medium heat. Add the garlic, onion, salt, and pepper and sauté, stirring frequently, for 2 minutes. Sprinkle with flour and stir to smooth out any lumps. Cook and stir for 1 minute.

Slowly pour in the milk and the wine or chicken stock, whisking constantly. Cook and stir for 3 minutes. Add the cream cheese and stir until melted. Remove the pan from the heat. Stir in the spinach and ¾ cup of the Parmesan cheese.

Mix the sauce and the vegetables in a large bowl and transfer to the casserole dish. Top with the remaining cheese and bake for 30 minutes.

# DESSERTS

*How sweet are your words to my taste, sweeter than honey to my mouth!*
—PSALM 119:103

Desserts warm your heart and comfort your soul. They express love and remind us of the sweetness in life. They are the grand finale to a special meal, the centerpiece of a birthday party, and the first thing to disappear at a potluck.

Desserts can evoke memories of holidays, special occasions, and sweet moments that made an ordinary day extraordinary.

A towering four-layer cake smothered with rich ganache and piled with shards of chocolate to celebrate a special occasion.

Fresh seasonal berries in a whipped cream cloud shared with friends on a warm summer night.

An old-fashioned pound cake to cheer a lonely neighbor.

Milk and cookies as a special after-school treat.

Vanilla bean ice cream melting into the cracks of a warm fruit crisp at the end of a family dinner.

Desserts also bring back sweet memories of cooking with loved ones. Every time you make Gramma's oatmeal cookies with your kids, you remember your grandmother and the special time you spent in her kitchen. And you create new treasured memories with your kids as you pass along a family recipe, continuing traditions from generation to generation.

Take time for dessert. Enjoy life's sweet moments. And spread a little sweetness to those around you. Start with sprinkles. Sprinkles cause uncontrollable smiling.

## Cakes, Cupcakes, and Cheesecake

Berries and Cream Layer Cake

Fallen Chocolate Soufflé

Hummingbird Cupcakes

Strawberry Cupcakes

Elvis Cupcakes

Chocolate Zucchini Snack Cake

Lemon Cheesecake

Dark Chocolate Strawberry Shortcake

## Pies, Tarts, Cobblers, and Crisps

Frozen Margarita Pie

Chocolate Peanut Butter Cream Pie

Key Lime Pie

Strawberry Cheesecake Pie

Fruit Tart

Easy Peach Cobbler

Caramel Apple Crisp

## Parfaits and Puddings

Cool and Creamy Banana Pudding

Tiramisu Parfaits

Rice Pudding

Chocolate Mousse

Pumpkin Dark Chocolate Bread Pudding with Caramel Sauce

Chocolate Grand Marnier Crème Brulee

Vanilla Spice Poached Pears with Maple Cream Sauce

## Bars and Cookies

Mini Pumpkin Chocolate-Chip Whoopie Pies

Glazed Pumpkin Spice Cookies

Peanut Butter and Jelly Bars

Nickerdoodles

# BERRIES AND CREAM LAYER CAKE

*This gorgeous, show-stopping cake is light, cool, and refreshing. It's incredibly easy to make, so it's perfect for beginners. I combine chocolate cake with raspberries, or vanilla cake with strawberries, because I think these flavors are perfect partners, but you can create your own masterpiece. Display your layers of deliciousness on a cake pedestal and prepare to be adored.*

**MAKES 8 TO 10 SERVINGS.**

1 (18.25-ounce) box vanilla or chocolate cake mix and the ingredients listed on the back of the box

4 ounces cream cheese, softened

½ cup confectioners' sugar

2 cups heavy cream

1 teaspoon vanilla extract

3 cups berries, plus more for garnish

Prepare the cake as directed on the package for two 9-inch cake layers. Cut the cooled cake layers in half to create four layers.

In a medium bowl beat the cream cheese and confectioners' sugar with a hand mixer or in a stand mixer until creamy. Add the heavy cream and vanilla and beat until stiff peaks form.

Place the first cake layer on a platter and spread one-fourth of the whipped cream mixture on top. Arrange ¼ of the berries over the whipped cream. Repeat with the remaining layers, decoratively arranging the berries on the top, then garnishing with additional whole berries. Icing the sides is optional.

# FALLEN CHOCOLATE SOUFFLÉ

*This is the one time you actually want your soufflé to fall. When the center falls during cooling, it creates a crackled crevice perfect for filling with a billowy cloud of whipped cream and sweet berries. Oh my! Heavenly.*

**MAKES 8 TO 10 SERVINGS.**

5 large eggs, separated

6 tablespoons butter, cut into cubes, plus extra for preparing pan

3 (4-ounce) bars 60% cocoa chocolate bars, chopped

½ teaspoon salt

3 teaspoons vanilla extract, divided

1 ¼ cup sugar, divided

¼ cup all-purpose flour

1 cup heavy cream

¼ cup confectioners' sugar

2 cups assorted berries

Place the egg yolks in a small bowl and leave the yolks at room temperature for 30 minutes. Put the whites in the refrigerator until ready to use.

Preheat the oven to 350 degrees. Butter a 9-inch springform pan and line the bottom with parchment paper, and rub butter on the paper.

Melt the chocolate and butter together over a double boiler or in the microwave, stirring frequently. Transfer chocolate to a large mixing bowl and cool.

When the chocolate is just barely warm, beat in the salt, 2 teaspoons of the vanilla, and ½ cup of the sugar. Add the egg yolks one at a time, beating until incorporated. Add the flour and beat for 30 seconds.

In a separate bowl beat the chilled egg whites until soft

*continued on next page*

peaks form with a hand mixer or in a stand mixer. Add ½ cup sugar and continue beating until you have stiff peaks. Gently fold a quarter of the whipped whites into the chocolate mixture until almost incorporated. Add another quarter and fold until almost incorporated. Add the remaining whites and fold until completely incorporated. Pour into the springform pan.

Bake for 35 to 45 minutes or until the cake has puffed up and is cracked on top and a toothpick inserted in the center comes out clean. Remove the pan from the oven and place on a cooling rack. Leave undisturbed to cool completely. As the cake cools, it will collapse, creating a sunken center.

In a medium bowl whip the cream with the remaining 1 teaspoon vanilla and the confectioners' sugar with a hand mixer or in a stand mixer until whipped cream consistency. Store in the refrigerator until ready to serve.

Clean the berries, remove any stems, and cut the larger berries in half or into quarters. Place in a bowl and mix with the remaining ¼ cup of sugar. Let sit for 30 minutes.

To serve, remove the cake from the springform pan and place on a serving platter. Fill the crater with whipped cream, and carefully spoon the berries on the whipped cream cloud.

> *Don't wait for a special occasion to bake a spectacular layer cake or make a fancy dessert for someone you love. Love is the special occasion. Celebrate it.*

# HUMMINGBIRD CUPCAKES

*Every family or region has their own special version of traditional dishes. But that's not the case with Hummingbird Cake. It is a Southern classic, and everyone makes it pretty much the same way. No one is certain how it got its name, but I like the explanation that it's because it is so good you can't help but hum with every delicious bite.*

*I did mess with the classic just a tiny bit, and I put my twist on it by making Hummingbird Cupcakes instead of the traditional layer cake. Who doesn't love a cupcake?*

**MAKES 24 TO 28 CUPCAKES.**

**CUPCAKES**

3 cups all-purpose flour

1 teaspoon baking soda

1 teaspoon salt

1 teaspoon ground cinnamon

2 cups sugar

3 large eggs, lightly beaten

1 cup vegetable oil

1 ½ teaspoons vanilla extract

1 (8-ounce) can crushed pineapple (do not drain)

2 cups mashed extra-ripe bananas

2 cups chopped, toasted pecans, divided

**CREAM CHEESE ICING**

½ cup (1 stick) butter, softened

1 (8-ounce) package cream cheese, softened

1 teaspoon vanilla extract

1 (16-ounce) box confectioners' sugar

*To make the cupcakes:*

Preheat the oven to 350 degrees. Line 2 ½ muffin tins with paper liners.

Whisk together the flour, baking soda, salt, and cinnamon in a large bowl until thoroughly combined. Stir in the sugar.

In a medium bowl combine the eggs, oil, and vanilla. Stir the egg mixture into the flour mixture. You will have a thick paste. Stir in the pineapple and bananas and 1 cup of the toasted pecans.

Fill the muffin cups two-thirds full with batter. Bake for 20 to 25 minutes or until a toothpick inserted into the center comes out clean

Remove tins from the oven and set on wire racks. After 10 minutes remove the cupcakes from the tins and let cool completely on wire racks.

*To make the icing:*

In a large bowl cream the butter and cream cheese together with a hand mixer or in a stand mixer until smooth and creamy. Beat in the vanilla. Once combined, add the confectioners' sugar and continue to beat until the icing comes together.

Ice the cooled cupcakes. Sprinkle the tops with the remaining toasted pecans.

# STRAWBERRY CUPCAKES

*No one can resist these very strawberry cupcakes. They are pretty enough to serve at a shower or Mother's Day brunch and so delicious men will wear white gloves and a bonnet so they don't miss out. This recipe works best with frozen and thawed berries in syrup, so you don't have to wait for strawberry season to enjoy them.*

*If you make a layer cake instead of cupcakes, consider adding a chocolate mousse filling (see page 219 for recipe). The result will amaze you and those you serve. Chocolate and strawberries scream LOVE!*

**MAKES 24 CUPCAKES.**

**CUPCAKES**

2 (10-ounce) packages frozen strawberries in syrup, thawed

4 large eggs, beaten

½ cup vegetable oil

¼ cup water

1 teaspoon vanilla extract

1 (16.25-ounce) box white cake mix

1 (3-ounce) box strawberry-flavored gelatin

**ICING**

1 (8-ounce) package cream cheese, softened

½ cup (1 stick) butter, softened

½ teaspoon vanilla extract

1 cup strawberries, hulled and chopped

6 to 8 cups confectioners' sugar, divided

Strawberries for garnishing, if desired

*To make the cupcakes:*

Preheat the oven to 350 degrees. Line 2 muffin tins with cupcake liners.

Puree the strawberries in syrup in a blender. Pour 1 ¼ cups of the puree into a large bowl, reserving the rest for the icing. Add the eggs, oil, water, and vanilla to the large bowl with the puree and beat for 1 minute with a hand mixer or in a stand mixer. Add the cake mix and gelatin and beat to combine. Fill the liners two-thirds full and bake for 18 to 22 minutes or until a toothpick inserted in the center comes out clean. Remove muffin tins from the oven and set on a wire rack to cool completely.

*To make the icing:*

Place the cream cheese, butter, and vanilla in the large bowl and beat until smooth and creamy with a hand mixer or in a stand mixer. Add the reserved puree and the chopped strawberries and beat until completely combined. Add 6 cups of the confectioners' sugar and beat until creamy. Add additional confectioners' sugar until you have an icing consistency. At this point you will, of course, dip your finger into the pink strawberriliciousness to make sure it tastes as yummy as it looks. You will then be compelled to grab a spoon. Just try to leave enough to ice the cupcakes.

Garnish iced cupcakes with strawberries, chocolate-covered strawberries, or a drizzle of chocolate.

# ELVIS CUPCAKES

*One day I had ten overripe bananas on my kitchen counter. Too many for just a couple of loaves of banana bread, so I had to come up with something else to do with them or shove them in the freezer to use later. Alas, my freezer was full, so Elvis Cupcakes were born.*

*Because peanut butter is the perfect partner for bananas, I made peanut butter icing for the cupcakes. Oh my! The icing was so good and I had made more than I needed, so I used the extra to ice a small purchased chocolate pound cake I cut into layers. I also ate some (more than some) with a spoon. And I spread some on graham crackers. And I may have licked the bowl. Hopefully no one noticed the icing in my hair.*

**MAKES APPROXIMATELY 20 CUPCAKES.**

## CUPCAKES

2 ⅓ cups all-purpose flour

1 teaspoon baking powder

½ teaspoon baking soda

1 teaspoon ground cinnamon

1 teaspoon salt

½ cup (1 stick) butter, softened

1 ¼ cups sugar

2 large eggs

¼ cup buttermilk

¼ cup honey

2 tablespoons vegetable oil

1 teaspoon vanilla extract

2 bananas, very ripe and mashed

½ cup mini semisweet chocolate chips

*To make the cupcakes:*

Preheat the oven to 350 degrees. Place the cupcake liners in a muffin tin. Lightly spray the liners with nonstick cooking spray.

In a medium bowl whisk together the flour, baking powder, baking soda, cinnamon, and salt. In a large bowl cream the butter and sugar with a hand mixer or in a stand mixer until smooth and creamy.

Add the eggs, one at a time, beating for 30 seconds after each addition. Add the buttermilk, honey, vegetable oil, and vanilla and continue beating until combined. Add the bananas and continue beating only until combined. Add the dry ingredients and beat until the batter is smooth. Stir in the chocolate chips.

Fill the muffin cups two-thirds full. Bake for 24 to 28 minutes or until a toothpick inserted in the center comes out clean. While the cupcakes are in the oven, sing a few lines of "All Shook Up" and shake your hips as a preemptive calorie-burning activity.

When the cupcakes are done, remove the tin from the oven and place on a wire rack for 10 minutes. Remove the cupcakes from the tin and place directly on the wire rack to cool completely.

*continued on next page*

### ICING

½ cup (1 stick) butter, softened

1 cup creamy peanut butter

1 teaspoon vanilla extract

¼ teaspoon salt

2 cups confectioners' sugar

⅓ cup heavy cream

*To make the icing:*

In a medium bowl cream together the butter and peanut butter with a hand mixer or in a stand mixer. Add the vanilla and salt and continue beating. Add the confectioners' sugar and beat until creamy. Slowly add the cream. You may need a little more to reach your desired consistency.

Ice the cooled cupcakes.

Pour yourself a tall glass of cold milk.

Grab a cupcake.

Now grab another.

Now you should probably stop.

NOTE: If you are going to pipe the icing onto the cupcakes instead of spreading it on, you will need to double the icing ingredients, as piping uses much more icing.

*When a birthday falls on a school day, make breakfast special by putting candles in waffles, pancakes, cinnamon rolls, or coffee cake. Starting the day by honoring the birthday boy or girl will encourage your child throughout the day and make waiting for the weekend celebration a little easier.*

# CHOCOLATE ZUCCHINI SNACK CAKE

*Zucchini manages to take over my vegetable garden every year. If I don't keep a close eye on them, before I know it I have zucchini the size of watermelons. It seems as if it happens overnight.*

*When my zucchini starts to get out of hand, I find if I shred them with a box grater I can sneak them into just about anything. I add zucchini to meatloaf, pasta dishes, casseroles, and even chocolate cake! This cake is so moist it doesn't need any icing. I dust it with confectioners' sugar, but more for decoration than taste.*

**MAKES 16 SERVINGS.**

½ cup (1 stick) butter, softened

½ cup vegetable oil

1 ¾ cups sugar

2 large eggs

½ cup buttermilk

1 teaspoon vanilla extract

2 ½ cups white whole wheat flour

¼ cup unsweetened cocoa powder

1 teaspoon baking soda

½ teaspoon baking powder

½ teaspoon salt

1 teaspoon ground cinnamon

Dash of ground cloves

2 cups shredded zucchini

¾ cup mini semisweet chocolate chips

Confectioners' sugar for garnish, optional

Preheat the oven to 325 degrees. Spray a 9 x 13-inch baking pan with nonstick cooking spray.

In a large bowl beat together the butter, oil, and sugar with a hand mixer or in a stand mixer. Add the eggs, buttermilk, and vanilla and continue beating until combined.

In a medium bowl whisk together the flour, cocoa powder, baking soda, baking powder, salt, cinnamon, and cloves. Add the flour mixture to the butter mixture and beat until combined. Stir in the zucchini and the chocolate chips.

Bake for 45 to 55 minutes or until a toothpick inserted into the center comes out clean. Remove from the oven and cool on a wire rack. Cut into squares and dust with confectioners' sugar if desired.

# LEMON CHEESECAKE

*After many years of experimenting, I have finally perfected the ultimate cheesecake. This lemon cheesecake is light and creamy instead of heavy and dense. The crust remains crisp even after a few days. And the lemon brightens the richness of the cheesecake. One bite will change your life.*

**MAKES 10 SERVINGS.**

## CRUST

2 cups graham cracker crumbs

⅓ cup sugar

½ cup (1 stick) butter, melted

## FILLING

4 (8-ounce) packages cream cheese, softened

1 ¼ cups sugar

1 ½ teaspoons vanilla extract

1 cup sour cream

1 (14-ounce) can sweetened condensed milk

⅓ cup freshly squeezed lemon juice

3 large eggs, room temperature

2 large egg yolks, room temperature

¼ cup all-purpose flour

Zest of 2 lemons

2 to 3 drops yellow food coloring, optional

## WHIPPED CREAM

1 cup heavy cream

¼ cup confectioners' sugar

1 teaspoon vanilla extract

2 large marshmallows

Berries and lemons for garnish if desired

*continued on next page*

*To make the crust:*

Preheat the oven to 375 degrees.

Combine the graham cracker crumbs, sugar, and butter in a medium bowl and press into the bottom and up the sides of a 9-inch springform pan. Bake for 6 minutes. Remove to cool.

*To make the filling:*

In a large bowl beat the cream cheese until creamy with a hand mixer or in a stand mixer. Add the sugar and beat for 1 minute. Add the vanilla, sour cream, sweetened condensed milk, lemon juice, eggs, and yolks and beat for 1 minute. Add the flour, lemon zest, and food coloring, if using, and beat just until combined.

Tear two 16-inch strips of foil and place one over the other to form a cross. Set the springform pan in the center of the foil, where the two pieces overlap. Gather the foil tightly up the sides of the springform pan to form a tight seal around the bottom edge of the pan.

Pour the filling into the crust. Set the pan inside a larger, shallow baking pan. Pour hot water into the larger pan so it's about a third of the way up the springform pan, being careful not to come up above the foil. Place in the oven. Bake for 20 minutes. Reduce the heat to 250 degrees and continue baking for 90 minutes or until the center is set but still looks wet. (It could take 2 hours.)

Remove the pan from the oven. Remove the springform pan from the water bath and place the pan on a wire rack to cool completely. Carefully run a sharp knife around the crust to separate it from the pan, and loosen the ring but don't remove it. Place the cheesecake in the refrigerator for 2 hours to chill.

*To make the whipped cream:*

Combine the heavy cream, confectioners' sugar, and vanilla in a medium bowl and beat until the mixture is almost whipped with a hand mixer or in a stand mixer. Place the two marshmallows on a paper plate and microwave on high for 10 to 15 seconds or until the marshmallows appear to expand like balloons. Quickly add the marshmallows to the whipped cream and continue beating just until the mixture reaches a whipped cream consistency.

When the cheesecake has chilled, remove the ring and transfer to a serving plate or cake stand. Pipe the whipped cream decoratively on the cheesecake as desired and garnish with berries and lemon slices or zest. Refrigerate for several hours or overnight before serving.

RECIPE TIPS: Always do the following to ensure even cooking, a creamy filling, a flat, even top, and no cracks:

- Cook at a low temperature for a longer period of time.
- Add a few tablespoons of all-purpose flour to the filling.
- Cook in a water bath.

# DARK CHOCOLATE STRAWBERRY SHORTCAKE

*Dark chocolate-covered strawberries are my very favorite dessert. I am also very fond of strawberry shortcake, so it made sense to combine these two loves. I was very happy with the results. Very, very happy.*

**MAKES 8 SERVINGS.**

### SHORTCAKES

2 cups all-purpose flour

¼ cup dark cocoa powder, sifted

⅓ cup sugar

2 teaspoons baking powder

1 teaspoon baking soda

½ teaspoon salt

½ of a 4-ounce bar 72% cocoa chocolate bar, finely chopped

½ cup (1 stick) plus 1 tablespoon butter, softened

¾ cup heavy cream

1 to 2 tablespoons raw sugar

### STRAWBERRIES

1 quart strawberries, sliced

¼ cup sugar (or to taste)

### WHIPPED CREAM

1 cup heavy cream

¼ cup confectioners' sugar

½ teaspoon vanilla extract

*To make the shortcakes:*

Preheat the oven to 450 degrees. Line a baking pan or cookie sheet with parchment paper.

In a large bowl combine the flour, cocoa powder, sugar, baking powder, baking soda, and salt with a whisk. Stir in the chopped chocolate. Cut in the stick of butter until you have coarse crumbs. Stir in the cream.

Plop 8 mounds of dough onto the prepared pan. Melt the additional 1 tablespoon of butter and brush over the tops. Sprinkle the raw sugar on top of each mound. Bake for 12–14 minutes or until a toothpick inserted in the center comes out clean.

Cool on a wire rack (not completely—these are really good when still a little warm).

*To prepare the berries:*

Combine the berries and sugar in a medium bowl and set aside for 30 minutes to allow the sugar to dissolve.

*To make the whipped cream:*

In a medium chilled bowl whip the cream with a hand mixer or in a stand mixer until it starts to thicken. Add the confectioners' sugar and vanilla and continue to beat until stiff peaks form. Keep cold.

*To assemble:*

Slice the shortcake in half. Spoon the whipped cream over the bottom half. Top with some berries and juices. Place the top half of the shortcake over the berries. Top with more berries. Garnish with more whipped cream and a drizzle of chocolate syrup (oh, why not?!).

I'm sorry.

And you're welcome.

# FROZEN MARGARITA PIE

*This frozen pie can be made ahead. It's a wonderfully cool and refreshing dessert for your summer cookouts, or to cool your tongue after a spicy meal. I love that it is sweet, salty, and tart all at the same time. You can also make a frozen strawberry daiquiri pie version. Simply replace the lime sherbet with strawberry sorbet, and replace the margarita mix with strawberry daiquiri mix. Garnish with strawberries. Tasty!*

**MAKES 8 SERVINGS.**

1 ¼ cups crushed pretzel sticks

¼ cup sugar

½ cup (1 stick) butter, melted

4 ½ cups vanilla ice cream

2 ½ cups lime sherbet

⅔ cup frozen margarita mix concentrate, thawed

3 tablespoons tequila, optional

Whipped cream or frozen whipped topping, thawed

Lime slices for garnish, optional

Spray a pie dish with butter-flavored nonstick cooking spray or "grease" with softened butter. Combine crushed pretzels, sugar, and butter in a medium bowl. Create a crust in the prepared pie dish by pressing the pretzel mixture into the bottom and up the sides. Freeze for 1 hour to set.

Let the ice cream and sherbet sit on the counter for 10 minutes to soften slightly. Stir the margarita mix into the vanilla ice cream. Mix the tequila (if using) into the lime sherbet. Place both mixtures in the freezer until almost firm. Drop spoonsful of lime sherbet over the top of the vanilla ice cream mixture. Gently fold together, just until you achieve a marbled effect. Immediately spoon the mixture into the pie shell. Cover with plastic wrap and place in the freezer for several hours.

To serve, remove the pie from the freezer and let stand to soften for 15 minutes. Garnish with whipped cream and lime slices. (A pretzel would be cute too.)

# CHOCOLATE PEANUT BUTTER CREAM PIE

*I think pies make people smile, so it's one of my favorite things to bring when someone needs some TLC. The recipient automatically feels loved on when you extend your arms with a pie in your hands.*

*While I love the feeling I get when I pull a pie out of the oven, I prefer baked fillings in the form of a crisp instead of a pie. My favorite pies are refrigerator pies. I love coconut cream, chocolate cream, cool and creamy strawberry cheesecake pie, and this chocolate peanut butter cream pie. You really can't go wrong when you combine chocolate and peanut butter, so I knew the combination would make a great pie. I was right. You will fall in love with this pie. It has a few steps but nothing very complicated.*

*I think you should make two. One for you and one for someone in need of some pie love.*

---

**MAKES 8 SERVINGS.**

**CRUST**

1 (9-ounce) package chocolate wafers

½ cup honey roasted peanuts

½ cup (1 stick) butter, melted

**CHOCOLATE GANACHE LAYER**

¾ cup dark chocolate chips

½ cup heavy cream

**PEANUT BUTTER CREAM LAYER**

1 (8-ounce) package cream cheese, softened

2 ¼ cups heavy cream, divided

⅓ cup sugar, divided

1 ½ teaspoons vanilla extract, divided

1 ¼ cups creamy peanut butter

1 banana, sliced

Chocolate curls, optional

⅓ cup honey roasted peanuts, coarsely chopped

**To make the crust:**

Preheat the oven to 350 degrees.

Lightly spray a pie dish with nonstick cooking spray.

Crush the wafers and nuts together in a food processor and place the crumbs in a medium bowl. Add the melted butter, stirring until combined. Transfer the crumb mixture to the pie dish and press up the sides and onto the bottom to form the crust.

Bake for 10 minutes. Remove to a wire rack and cool completely before filling.

**To make the chocolate ganache:**

Place the chocolate chips in a medium bowl. Pour the cream into a small saucepan over medium-low heat and bring almost to the boiling point. Pour over the chips. Let the chips sit in the hot cream for 5 minutes, and then stir until smooth and glossy. Pour into the cooled crust. Place in the refrigerator for 45 minutes to set the layer.

**To make the peanut butter layer:**

Place the cream cheese, ¼ cup cream, ⅓ cup of the confectioners' sugar, and 1 teaspoon vanilla in a large bowl and beat with a hand mixer or a stand mixer on medium speed for 60 seconds. Add the peanut butter and beat until completely combined.

*continued on next page*

In a medium bowl use clean beaters to whip 1 cup of the heavy cream until stiff peaks form. Fold ¼ of the whipped cream into the peanut butter mixture until combined. Fold in half of the remaining whipped cream until combined. Add the rest of the whipped cream and stir until completely incorporated. Resist the urge to stick your face in it. That would be messy and very hard to explain.

*To assemble:*

Spread a ½-inch layer of the peanut butter mixture over the chocolate layer. Arrange the banana slices over the peanut butter layer. Top with the remaining peanut butter mixture.

In a clean medium bowl use clean beaters to whip the remaining 1 cup heavy cream with the 3 tablespoons confectioners' sugar and ½ teaspoon vanilla until stiff peaks form. Spread over the pie.

Garnish the pie with chocolate curls and chopped nuts.

Cover and refrigerate for several hours or overnight before serving.

NOTE: I also make this pie using crushed chocolate sandwich cookies in place of the bananas. You will need about 10 cookies plus a few for garnishing the pie.

*A beautiful dessert makes a spectacular centerpiece to your table. It's a teaser that will have your family, friends, and guests anticipating what is to come, and eager to linger at the table just a bit longer.*

# KEY LIME PIE

*This is my favorite key lime pie. Period. I love the combination of the crisp, slightly sweet homemade graham cracker crust with the smooth, tart filling. The cool and creamy layer of fresh whipped cream completes this trifecta of perfection.*

**MAKES 8 SERVINGS.**

1 ¼ cup graham cracker crumbs

3 tablespoons sugar

⅓ cup butter, melted

4 large egg yolks

Zest of 2 limes (or 6 key limes)

1 (14-ounce) can sweetened condensed milk

⅔ cup key lime juice (fresh or bottled)

1 cup heavy cream

3 tablespoons confectioners' sugar

1 teaspoon vanilla extract

2 large marshmallows

2 limes sliced for garnish if desired

Preheat the oven to 350 degrees.

Combine the graham cracker crumbs, sugar, and butter and press into the bottom and up the sides of a 9-inch pie dish. Bake for 8 minutes. Let cool completely on a wire rack before filling.

Reduce the oven temperature to 325 degrees.

In a large bowl beat the egg yolks and lime zest with a hand mixer or in a stand mixer for 5 minutes or until the yolks are pale yellow and fluffy. Slowly drizzle in the sweetened condensed milk as you continue to beat for 3 minutes. Drizzle in the lime juice and beat for another minute.

Pour the mixture into the cooled crust and bake for 15 to 20 minutes or until set. Remove and cool completely on a wire rack. Place in the refrigerator to cool for 30 minutes.

Combine the heavy cream, confectioners' sugar, and vanilla in a medium bowl and beat with a hand mixer or in a stand mixer until almost whipped cream consistency. Place the two marshmallows on a paper plate and microwave on high for 10 to 15 seconds or until the marshmallows appear to expand like balloons. Quickly add to the whipped cream and continue beating just until it becomes a whipped cream consistency.

Spoon over the pie filling. Garnish with lime zest and lime slices if desired. Cover and refrigerate until ready to serve.

RECIPE TIP: Freshly whipped cream will collapse within hours, making it impossible to smooth on top of a dessert in advance. Adding the marshmallows stabilizes the whipped cream so you can "ice" a pie or other dessert a day in advance. The marshmallows will not change the flavor or texture of the whipped cream.

# STRAWBERRY CHEESECAKE PIE

*I make several of these during strawberry season. This cool and creamy pie is not as heavy or dense as a classic cheesecake, but it will still satisfy a cheesecake craving.*

*If you are short on time, you can always purchase a ready-made graham cracker crust, but I promise you, you will not regret the time put into a homemade crust. It truly makes the pie.*

**MAKES 8 SERVINGS.**

1 ½ cups graham cracker crumbs

¼ cup sugar

¼ cup (½ stick) butter, melted

2 cups sliced strawberries, plus more for garnish, divided

2 tablespoons sugar

1 (8-ounce) package cream cheese, softened

½ teaspoon vanilla extract

Dash of ground nutmeg

1 (8-ounce) container frozen whipped topping, thawed

Extra berries and melted dark chocolate chips for garnish

Preheat the oven to 375 degrees.

Combine the cracker crumbs and sugar in a medium bowl. Stir in the melted butter. Firmly pat the crumb mixture into the bottom and up the sides of a pie dish. Bake for 8 minutes. Remove from the oven and cool completely on a wire rack.

Place 1 ½ cups of the sliced strawberries in a small bowl and mash them with a potato masher. Mix with the sugar and set aside.

In a large bowl beat the cream cheese with the vanilla and nutmeg with a hand mixer or in a stand mixer until smooth and creamy. Add the crushed strawberries and blend well. Fold in the remaining ½ cup of the sliced berries and the whipped topping. Spoon the mixture into the cooled pie crust.

Refrigerate for about 1 hour and then garnish with sliced strawberries and drizzled chocolate or with chocolate-covered strawberries.

Cover and refrigerate overnight.

**NOTE:** If you are a chocoholic, replace the graham cracker crumbs with chocolate wafer cookie crumbs. The regular graham crackers give this pie more of a traditional cheesecake flavor and the chocolate crust gives it more of a chocolate-covered strawberry flavor.

# FRUIT TART

*I love serving this delicious fruit tart during summer months when fruit and berries are at their peak. The tart is so pretty it looks like something you would see in the display case of a fancy patisserie. In fact, you should probably leave some dirty dishes in the sink as proof you made it yourself. Maybe smear some flour on your face as added evidence. It's good to cover your bases.*

**MAKES 10 SERVINGS.**

1 cup ground walnuts

1 ½ cups all-purpose flour

3 tablespoons sugar

½ cup (1 stick) butter, softened

1 large egg yolk

1 teaspoon vanilla extract

1 (8-ounce) package cream cheese, softened

½ cup sugar

3 teaspoons vanilla extract, divided

1 ½ cups heavy cream

⅓ cup confectioners' sugar

Assorted fruit

¼ cup seedless berry-flavored jam or jelly

Preheat the oven to 350 degrees. Combine the walnuts, flour, sugar, butter, egg yolk, and vanilla in a medium bowl. Press the mixture onto the bottom and up the sides of a 12- or 13-inch tart pan.

Bake for 25 minutes or until the crust begins to brown. Remove from the oven and cool completely on a wire rack.

In a medium bowl beat the cream cheese, sugar, and 2 teaspoons of the vanilla with a hand mixer or in a stand mixer until smooth. In a separate medium bowl whip the heavy cream, confectioners' sugar, and remaining 1 teaspoon vanilla until stiff peaks form. Stir the whipped cream into the cream cheese mixture. Spread evenly in the cooled crust.

To serve, decoratively arrange the fruit over the cream filling. Melt the jam with 1 teaspoon water and brush it over the fruit to make it shine.

*Fruit Tart (above; page 210)*

*Easy Peach Cobbler (below; page 212)*

# EASY PEACH COBBLER

*I have visited more Southern and soul food restaurants than I can count, and I am here to tell you, no Southerner would dream of leaving without partaking in a little something sweet. You may not see the cook, but you instinctively know the owner's ma-maw is back in the kitchen, making secret recipes passed down from her own ma-maw. It would be rude and hurtful to leave without enjoying the fruits of her labor.*

*Nine times out of ten, whoever I am dining with orders banana pudding. Not me. I think my Cool and Creamy Banana Pudding (page 215) is the best ever, so I don't waste my time on the baked Southern version. For me it has to be peach cobbler. Ma-Maw is back in that kitchen, filling her well-seasoned cast-iron casserole dish with fresh peaches and sweet, buttery topping. Mercy! I don't know Ma-Maw, but I love her. I love her so very much.*

*When I have a craving for peach cobbler in the middle of winter, I put this very simple shortcut version together using frozen and jarred peaches. I use the basic formula of a dump cake. It gets me through until peach season rolls around and Ma-Maw is back in her kitchen!*

---

**MAKES 8 SERVINGS.**

1 (16-ounce) package frozen peaches, thawed

1 (24.5-ounce) jar sliced peaches in light syrup

¼ cup sugar

1 teaspoon ground cinnamon

⅛ teaspoon ground nutmeg

1 (18.25-ounce) package yellow cake mix

½ cup (1 stick) butter, cut into small cubes

⅓ cup firmly packed brown sugar

⅔ cup chopped pecans

Ice cream or whipped cream for serving

Preheat the oven to 350 degrees. Spray a 9 x 13-inch baking pan with nonstick cooking spray.

In a large bowl combine the peaches, sugar, cinnamon, and nutmeg. Transfer the mixture to the baking pan. Cover the peaches with the dry cake mix. Place the cubes of butter evenly over the top of the cake mix. Sprinkle with the brown sugar and then the pecans.

Bake for 1 hour or until golden brown on top and the edges are bubbling.

Serve warm with ice cream or whipped cream. (Dust ice cream or whipped cream with a little nutmeg for extra taste. It also adds to your presentation.)

# CARAMEL APPLE CRISP

*I love, love, love the aroma of anything with apples and cinnamon baking in the oven. The scent that fills your home as this delectable dessert bakes should be bottled. And this crisp will be one of the best you will ever eat. Oh. My. Goodness. It's caramel apple crisp bliss.*

**MAKES 8 SERVINGS.**

1 teaspoon ground cinnamon

1 (12.25-ounce) jar caramel ice-cream topping

6 Granny Smith apples, peeled, cored, and thinly sliced

⅔ cup all-purpose flour

½ cup firmly packed brown sugar

½ cup (1 stick) plus 2 tablespoons butter, cold and cut into cubes

⅔ cup quick-cooking oatmeal

½ cup chopped pecans

Whipped cream or vanilla ice cream for serving

Preheat the oven to 350 degrees. Spray an 8- or 9-inch square baking pan with nonstick cooking spray and set aside.

In a large bowl stir the cinnamon into the caramel sauce. Stir the apples into the caramel mixture and spoon into the baking pan. (The pan will be very full, but the apples will cook down.)

In a medium bowl mix the flour and brown sugar together with a wire whisk. Cut in the ½ cup cold butter with a pastry blender until the mixture looks like coarse crumbs. Stir in the oats and the pecans. Pour the mixture evenly over the apples. Dot with the remaining 2 tablespoons butter.

Bake for about 45 minutes or until the top is golden and the apples are tender. Remove from the oven and let sit for about 30 minutes.

Serve warm with whipped cream or vanilla ice cream. (I like to sprinkle a light dusting of cinnamon around the crisp and over the ice cream. It tastes yummy and makes your dish look extra special.)

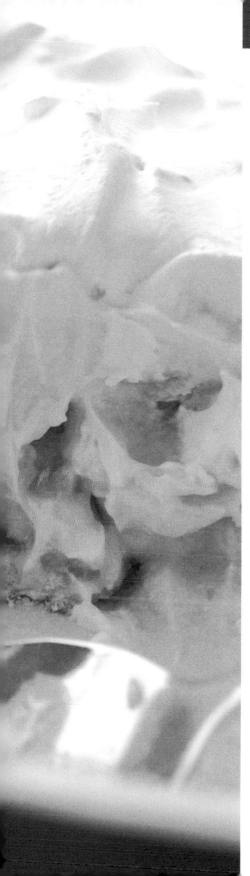

# COOL AND CREAMY BANANA PUDDING

*My favorite banana pudding recipe is the one my mom has been making since I was in middle school. I've never found a recipe I liked as well as this one, and everyone who tastes it feels the same way. They toss their grandmother's traditional baked version out the window and never look back.*

*This banana pudding gets raves every time I bring it to a potluck or take it to a family along with a hot meal. When I bring it to church functions, it's always one of the first things to go. Give it a chance. People will throw rose petals at your feet.*

**MAKES 8 TO 10 SERVINGS.**

3 (3.4-ounce) boxes instant vanilla pudding

5 cups 2% or whole milk

1 cup sour cream

1 (11-ounce) box vanilla wafers

About 6 bananas (ripe but not too ripe—this is better if your bananas aren't starting to turn brown)

1 (8-ounce) carton frozen whipped topping, thawed

In a large bowl combine the instant pudding, milk, and sour cream and whisk until smooth. Set aside to thicken.

Once the pudding has thickened (about 5 minutes) you can assemble your banana pudding.

Cover the bottom of a 9 x 13-inch casserole dish with a single layer of vanilla wafers. Slice the bananas and cover each cookie with a banana slice. Spoon a third of the pudding over the bananas. Repeat the layers two more times. Cover the third layer with the whipped topping. Cover with plastic wrap (use toothpicks to keep the wrap from sticking to the topping) and refrigerate overnight.

Try not to eat it all at once!

# TIRAMISU PARFAITS

*It's easy to turn just about any dessert into a parfait. It's as simple as changing the way you serve it and making each ingredient small enough to fit into the parfait glass. Crumble chocolate cake and layer it in individual parfait glasses with whipped cream and berries. Layer my Cool and Creamy Banana Pudding (page 215) in parfait glasses instead of assembling it in a baking dish. Turn any refrigerator pie into a parfait by crumbling the crust and alternating the crumbles with the pie filling and topping. The possibilities are endless.*

*For these Tiramisu Parfaits I took each element of the classic Italian dessert and layered them in parfait glasses. I wanted to present each of my dinner guests with an individual dessert, and dinner was Italian, so this made sense. It was the perfect ending to a perfect meal.*

---

**MAKES 6 PARFAITS.**

1 (8-ounce) container mascarpone cheese, softened

¼ cup confectioners' sugar

1 teaspoon vanilla extract

1 cup heavy cream

5 tablespoons coffee-flavored liqueur

1 (1.5-ounce) bar dark chocolate

1 (3-ounce) package ladyfingers

1 cup strong coffee, cooled

In a medium bowl beat the mascarpone cheese, sugar, and vanilla with a hand mixer or in a stand mixer until smooth and creamy. Add the heavy cream and beat until it becomes a whipped cream consistency. Add the liqueur and beat just until combined.

Grate about half of the bar of chocolate.

Tear the ladyfingers into pieces and divide half of the pieces among parfait glasses. Drizzle approximately 2 tablespoons of coffee over the ladyfingers. Divide half of the mascarpone cream among the 6 parfait glasses and sprinkle each with a layer of grated chocolate. Repeat with another layer of ladyfingers, coffee, and mascarpone cream.

Use a vegetable peeler to shave the rest of the chocolate bar into small curls and shavings. Top each parfait with the curls. Cover and refrigerate for at least 3 hours before serving.

# RICE PUDDING

*I didn't grow up eating rice pudding, but for some reason I feel nostalgic each time I make it. It's like a hug in a bowl. I love the creamy consistency, the sweetness, and the hint of cinnamon and nutmeg. I love the way it makes me feel.*

*You can serve this warm, at room temperature, or you can refrigerate it and eat it cold. It's delicious every way. Of this I am an expert. I lick the pot and the spoon while it's still warm. I take a few bites for "quality control" after spooning it into individual serving dishes. And of course I eat a serving after it sets up in the refrigerator. Maybe two servings.*

---

**MAKES 6 TO 8 SERVINGS.**

3 cups whole milk

1 ¼ cups water

2 tablespoons butter

½ teaspoon salt

3 cinnamon sticks, plus extra for garnish

1 cup short-grain rice

1 (14-ounce) can sweetened condensed milk

2 teaspoons pure vanilla extract

½ cup raisins

⅛ teaspoon ground nutmeg, plus more for garnish

Add the milk, water, butter, salt, and cinnamon sticks to a large saucepan and bring to a slow simmer over medium-low heat. Stir in the rice. Keep at a low simmer for 20 to 30 minutes or until the rice is tender, stirring occasionally to keep it from sticking on the bottom.

While the rice is simmering, combine the sweetened condensed milk, vanilla, raisins, and nutmeg in a small bowl. Set aside until needed. (This softens up the raisins.)

When the rice is tender, remove the cinnamon sticks and then stir in the raisin mixture. Return to a slow simmer and cook for 10 more minutes, stirring frequently. (It should be a pudding-like consistency. If it is runny, simmer a few minutes longer. It will also thicken as it cools so you don't want it to simmer too long and get it too thick.)

Remove from the heat. Let sit for 15 minutes and then pour the pudding into a large serving container or individual serving dishes. Garnish with a light sprinkling of nutmeg and a cinnamon stick.

You can serve the pudding warm or at room temperature, or cover and refrigerate until ready to serve cold.

# CHOCOLATE MOUSSE

*I love this recipe because it is super simple and because you don't use raw eggs as you would if you were making an authentic French recipe. It is just as delicious and elegant as the mousse you would be served in a fancy restaurant but without all the work.*

*You can serve the mousse in a glass dish, a wine glass, a chocolate shell, or use it as a filling for your favorite layer cake. It's rich, creamy, silky, and smooth. Just a few bites will satisfy the sweetest sweet tooth or the fiercest chocolate craving.*

**MAKES 6 TO 8 SERVINGS.**

2 cups heavy cream, divided
1 cup dark chocolate chips
½ teaspoon vanilla extract
2 tablespoons confectioners' sugar

Heat ½ cup of the heavy cream in a microwave-safe cup and microwave on high for 1 minute or until very hot to the touch. Put the chocolate chips in a large bowl and pour the hot cream over the chips. Set aside for 5 minutes.

Pour the remaining 1 ½ cups heavy cream into a large bowl. Add the vanilla and confectioners' sugar and beat with a hand mixer or in a stand mixer until stiff peaks form.

Stir the chocolate cream mixture until you have a smooth and creamy mixture and set aside to cool for 20 minutes. Now do your best not to eat the entire bowl with a spoon. It will be tempting, but don't do it. (Okay, maybe a little lick . . . just not the entire bowl.)

Gently fold one quarter of the whipped cream into the chocolate mixture. Add another quarter of the whipped cream and fold into the chocolate. Add the remaining whipped cream and fold until combined.

At this point you can put the mixture into a piping bag and pipe into chocolate shells or spoon the mixture into individual pudding cups or wine glasses. Cover and chill. Garnish with berries, whipped cream, chocolate curls, etc.

Now you can lick the bowl!

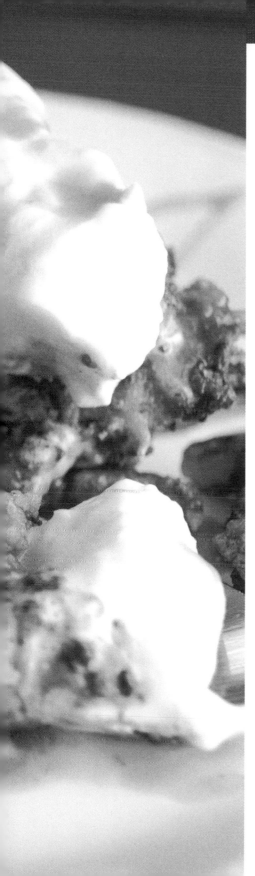

# PUMPKIN DARK CHOCOLATE BREAD PUDDING WITH CARAMEL SAUCE

*Pumpkin and chocolate is a classic combination like peanut butter and jelly, spaghetti and meatballs, eighties music and big hair . . .*

*This bread pudding is a wonderful and unique holiday dessert. I would much rather have this than pumpkin pie. Make it just one time and you may never go back to the pie.*

**MAKES 8 TO 10 SERVINGS.**

1 (16-ounce) loaf brown sugar cinnamon swirl bread (open one end of the package about 8 hours earlier so the bread will be slightly stale)
3 large eggs
1 cup heavy cream
¾ cup milk
1 cup canned pumpkin
½ cup brown sugar
1 teaspoon vanilla extract
Scant teaspoon pumpkin pie spice
¼ teaspoon salt
½ cup (1 stick) butter, melted
1 cup dark chocolate chips
½ cup chopped pecans
Caramel Sauce (recipe follows)

Cut the bread into 1-inch cubes and set aside. Spray a 9 x 13-inch casserole dish with nonstick cooking spray.

In a large bowl whisk together the eggs, cream, milk, pumpkin, brown sugar, vanilla, pumpkin pie spice, and salt. In another large bowl combine the bread cubes and butter and stir to coat. Stir in the chocolate chips, and then add the egg mixture, stirring to combine. Transfer to the casserole dish. Let sit for 15 minutes.

*continued on next page*

Preheat the oven to 325 degrees.

After 15 minutes, sprinkle the top of the bread pudding with the chopped pecans and place the baking dish in the oven. Bake for 50 minutes or until set in the center. Remove from the oven and let rest for 20 minutes.

To serve, drizzle with caramel sauce. (You can also serve with vanilla ice cream.)

## CARAMEL SAUCE

*This is an easy and delicious go-to caramel sauce that you can use on anything that you think needs a little caramel.*

½ cup (1 stick) butter
½ cup heavy cream
½ cup brown sugar
½ teaspoon pure vanilla extract

Combine the butter, cream, and brown sugar in a saucepan and place over low heat to melt the butter. As soon as the butter is melted, increase the heat so that the mixture comes to a gentle boil. Boil for 5 minutes, stirring frequently. Remove from the heat and let sit for 5 minutes. Stir in the vanilla and then set aside to cool and thicken.

*Baking is a way to extend your heart to others in times of need.*

# CHOCOLATE GRAND MARNIER CRÈME BRULEE

*Fancy schmancy! When I make crème brulee I let everyone torch their own. It's so much fun and a great way to get everyone into the kitchen together—even the kids. Just keep an eye on the torch! Adult supervision is imperative for children's safety and for the protection of poor Kitty's tail. Trust me. A torch in the hands of a ten-year-old turns everything in the kitchen into an experiment.*

SPECIAL EQUIPMENT: A crème brulee or kitchen torch

**MAKES APPROXIMATELY 12 SERVINGS.**

2 (4-ounce) bars 60% cocoa chocolate, chopped

4 cups heavy cream

2 teaspoons vanilla extract

3 tablespoons Grand Marnier

2 tablespoons dark cocoa powder

9 large egg yolks

½ cup sugar

1 tablespoon orange zest

12 tablespoons raw sugar

Preheat the oven to 300 degrees.

Place the chocolate pieces in a heatproof bowl. Heat the cream in a saucepan over medium heat just to the boiling point and pour over the chocolate. Let sit for 5 minutes. Stir until smooth. Add the vanilla, Grand Marnier, and cocoa powder.

In a medium bowl beat the egg yolks with the sugar and orange zest for 90 seconds. Whisk a few spoonsful of the warm chocolate mixture into the egg yolks, whisking constantly. Repeat with another few spoonsful before adding the remaining chocolate. Once all is incorporated and smooth, pour into individual ramekins and place in a large baking pan with 2- to 3-inch sides. Pour hot water into the baking pan until the water level is about halfway up the sides of the ramekins. Carefully transfer the pan to the oven and bake for 45 to 50 minutes or until set.

Remove the ramekins from the water and place on a wire rack until completely cool. Cover and refrigerate for 6 hours or overnight.

To serve, sprinkle 1 tablespoon of the raw sugar evenly over each ramekin. Use the torch to caramelize the sugar and form the crust.

# VANILLA SPICE POACHED PEARS WITH MAPLE CREAM SAUCE

*Simple. Gorgeous. Delectable. Poached pears are like dessert art. Imagine the oohs and aahs when you present a perfectly plated poached pear with maple cream sauce before each dinner guest. It's easier than you may think!*

**MAKES 6 SERVINGS.**

Juice of 1 lemon

6 ripe but still firm Bosc pears with stems

4 cups apple juice

4 cups water

⅔ cup light brown sugar

2 cinnamon sticks

1 vanilla bean, halved lengthwise

1 teaspoon whole cloves

¼ teaspoon ground nutmeg

Maple Cream Sauce (recipe follows)

⅔ cup chopped toasted pecans

Squeeze the lemon juice into a large bowl of water. Slice a thin sliver off the bottom of the pears so they can stand when serving. Peel the pears, leaving the stems on. As you peel the pears, place them in the bowl of lemon water to keep them from browning.

In a pot large enough to stand all of the pears, combine the apple juice, water, brown sugar, cinnamon sticks, vanilla bean, cloves, and nutmeg. Carefully stand the pears in the poaching liquid. Bring to a simmer over medium heat, reducing the heat if the liquid begins to boil too rapidly. Simmer for 30 minutes or until just tender. Remove from the heat and let the pears cool in the poaching liquid.

While the pears are cooling, prepare the Maple Cream Sauce.

To serve, stand each pear on a dessert plate and drizzle with Maple Cream Sauce. Sprinkle with toasted pecans.

**MAPLE CREAM SAUCE**

½ cup heavy cream

¾ cup brown sugar

4 tablespoons butter

2 teaspoons vanilla extract

2 tablespoons pure maple syrup

Combine the cream, brown sugar, and butter in a small saucepan over medium-low heat. Bring to a low simmer and cook, stirring frequently, for 5 minutes or until the sauce begins to thicken. Remove from the heat and stir in the vanilla and maple syrup.

# MINI PUMPKIN CHOCOLATE-CHIP WHOOPIE PIES

*Whoopie pies are just plain adorable, and it's pretty fun to say, "whoopie pie." I make these miniature-size so you get a bite of sweetness without going overboard. They are ridiculously good, so you will need to show some restraint.*

**MAKES 18 TO 20 MINI WHOOPIE PIES.**

**COOKIES**

6 tablespoons butter, softened

⅔ cup brown sugar

½ cup sugar

1 cup canned pumpkin puree

1 teaspoon vanilla extract

2 large eggs

2 cups all-purpose flour

1 teaspoon baking powder

½ teaspoon baking soda

¾ teaspoon salt

1 teaspoon pumpkin pie spice

⅔ cup mini semisweet chocolate chips

**FILLING**

1 ½ cups cream cheese, softened

½ cup heavy cream

½ teaspoon vanilla extract

½ cup confectioners' sugar

*To make the cookies:*

Preheat the oven to 375 degrees. Line cookie sheets with parchment paper. (Depending on the size of your cookie sheets, you will end up with approximately 4 batches of 9.)

In a large bowl beat together the butter, brown sugar, and sugar with a hand mixer or in a stand mixer until smooth and creamy. Add the pumpkin, vanilla, and eggs and continue to beat until well incorporated.

In a medium bowl whisk together the flour, baking powder, baking soda, salt, and pumpkin pie spice. Add the flour mixture to the butter mixture and continue to beat for 1 minute. Stir in the chocolate chips.

Spoon heaping tablespoons of batter onto the parchment paper–lined cookie sheets. Place them about 1 ½ to 2 inches apart. Bake for 12 minutes or until puffed up and dry on top. Remove from the oven and let cool on the cookie sheets for 5 minutes before removing with a spatula to wire racks.

Repeat until all of the batter has been used.

*To make the filling:*

In a medium bowl beat the cream cheese for 1 minute with a hand mixer or in a stand mixer. Add the heavy cream and vanilla. Beat until combined. Add the confectioners' sugar and beat until the mixture is smooth, about 30 to 60 seconds.

*To assemble:*

Spoon a heaping tablespoon of filling on one half of the cookies. Top with the remaining halves. Store in the refrigerator in an airtight container . . . unless you eat them all in one sitting, which is a definite possibility.

# GLAZED PUMPKIN SPICE COOKIES

*These are similar to oatmeal cookies but a little softer and less chewy because of the pumpkin. They are absolutely wonderful without the glaze, but it's the glaze that makes them really special.*

**MAKES 3 TO 4 DOZEN COOKIES.**

### COOKIES

2 cups all-purpose flour

1 ⅓ cups quick-cooking oats

1 teaspoon baking soda

1 teaspoon salt

1 teaspoon ground cinnamon

⅛ teaspoon ground nutmeg

1 cup butter

1 cup sugar

1 cup firmly packed light brown sugar

1 cup pumpkin puree

1 ½ teaspoons vanilla extract

1 large egg

1 cup raisins

1 cup chopped pecans

### GLAZE

¼ cup (½ stick) butter

2 ounces cream cheese, softened

½ teaspoon vanilla extract

½ cup confectioners' sugar, sifted

⅛ teaspoon ground cinnamon

Dash of ground allspice

Dash of ground nutmeg

*To make the cookies:*

Preheat the oven to 350 degrees. Lightly spray cookie sheets with nonstick cooking spray.

In a medium bowl whisk together the flour, oats, baking soda, salt, cinnamon, and nutmeg.

In a large bowl beat the butter with the sugars with a hand mixer or in a stand mixer until creamy. Add the pumpkin, vanilla, and egg, beating just until combined. Stir in the raisins and pecans.

Drop by spoonsful, about 2 inches apart, onto the cookie sheets. Press down lightly to spread a little. (Cookies will spread more while cooking.)

Bake for approximately 17 minutes. Check them at 15 minutes, as oven temperatures vary. Remove the cookie sheets from the oven and let sit for 2 to 3 minutes before removing the cookies to a wire rack to cool completely.

*To make the glaze:*

Melt the butter in a medium microwavable bowl and stir in the cream cheese to combine. Add the vanilla, confectioners' sugar, cinnamon, allspice, and nutmeg. Taste. Add a dash more allspice and/or nutmeg if you think it needs it. Just don't overdo it. You don't want the spicy glaze to overpower the rest of the flavors.

Line up the cooled cookies on waxed paper–lined cookies sheets on your countertop. Drizzle the glaze over the cookies in long strokes, drizzling across several cookies at a time for the best effect. Place the cookie sheets in the refrigerator to set the glaze. This should take about 30 minutes. Remove and store the cookies in a sealed container.

# PEANUT BUTTER AND JELLY BARS

*These bars are the perfect after-school treat on the first day back to school after summer break. They also make great lunchbox treats. But don't rule out big kids. Everyone loves peanut butter and jelly!*

*You can use any flavor of jam, but berry flavors work best. Try black raspberry, blackberry, or marionberry.*

**MAKES 16 TO 20 BARS.**

1 cup butter, softened

¾ cup sugar

½ cup firmly packed light brown sugar

1 (18-ounce) jar creamy peanut butter

2 large eggs, softened

2 teaspoons vanilla extract

2 ½ cups all-purpose flour

½ cup rolled oats

1 teaspoon salt

1 teaspoon baking powder

1 (10-ounce) jar seedless jam

1 cup honey roasted peanuts, chopped

Preheat the oven to 350 degrees. Spray a 9 x 13-inch baking pan with nonstick cooking spray.

In a large bowl cream together the butter and sugars with a hand mixer or in a stand mixer until smooth and fluffy. Add the peanut butter and beat until combined. Add the eggs and vanilla and beat for 30 seconds.

In a medium bowl combine the flour, oats, salt, and baking powder with a whisk to sift. Add the flour mixture to the peanut butter mixture and beat until completely incorporated.

Spread two-thirds of the dough into the bottom of the baking pan. Warm the jam for about 10 seconds in the microwave to make it easier to spread, and then spread evenly over the peanut butter dough. Drop small pieces of the remaining dough over the jam layer. Sprinkle with the chopped peanuts.

Bake for 45 to 50 minutes or until golden brown. Cool completely before cutting into squares.

# NICKERDOODLES

*Snickerdoodles have been Nick's favorite cookie since he was two years old, so I lovingly refer to them as "Nickerdoodles." I've tried lots of recipes and even purchased the three-dollar-per-cookie fancy ones from the bakery, but this is the one he wants. That makes my momma heart happy.*

**MAKES 4 DOZEN COOKIES.**

2 ¾ cups all-purpose flour

2 teaspoons cream of tarter

1 teaspoon baking soda

¼ teaspoon salt

1 cup butter, softened

1 ½ cups plus 8 tablespoons sugar

2 large eggs

½ teaspoon vanilla extract

8 teaspoons ground cinnamon

Preheat the oven to 350 degrees.

In a medium bowl whisk together the flour, cream of tartar, baking soda, and salt. In a large bowl cream the butter and 1 ½ cups of the sugar with a hand mixer or in a stand mixer. Add the eggs and vanilla and continue beating until combined. Add the flour mixture and beat on low speed until incorporated.

In a shallow dish mix the cinnamon into the remaining 8 tablespoons sugar. Roll the dough into 1-inch balls, and then roll in the cinnamon-sugar mixture to coat. Place the dough 2 inches apart on a cookie sheet. Bake for 12 minutes or until golden around the edges.

Let the cookies sit on the cookie sheet for 3 minutes before removing to a wire rack to cool completely.

# REACHING OUT AND GATHERING IN

## IDEAS FOR REACHING OUT TO THOSE IN NEED
## AND GATHERING IN WITH THOSE YOU LOVE

"You must love the LORD your God with all your heart, all your soul,
and all your mind." This is the first and greatest commandment. A
second is equally important: "Love your neighbor as yourself."
—MATTHEW 22:37–39 NLT

As a food blogger I think quite a lot about food. I wait with anticipation for the next month's issues of my favorite food magazines. I spend way too much time watching food channels. I create recipes in my mind as I fall asleep at night. My butcher and I are on a first-name basis. I have every aisle of my grocery store memorized. And I am happiest when I'm in my kitchen, elbow-deep in flour amid a cloud of confectioners' sugar dust, cooking for those I love and those God places on my heart.

Cooking for people makes me happy. The dirty dishes that result, well . . . not so much. But it's worth the smile on Nick's face when I pull a pan of his favorite "Nickerdoodles" out of the oven; the look of joy in a friend's eyes when I walk in with a warm caramel apple crisp; or the audible sigh of relief when I deliver a ready-for-the-oven casserole to an overwhelmed mother of five.

Whether reaching out to neighbors or gathering with our family around the table, a pan of lasagna or a warm coffee cake ready to share is a tangible way to show love and share grace with those around us.

# REACHING OUT

Twenty years from now, you'll be more disappointed by the
things you didn't do than the ones you did do.
—MARK TWAIN

When a friend, neighbor, or coworker is struggling, it's sometimes hard for that person to acknowledge the struggle or to ask for help. I know. I've been there. The last few months of my husband's life were painful emotionally, and they were physically difficult as well. Not only was I Ron's caregiver, but I was the mother of a three-year-old boy who didn't understand what was happening to his daddy.

But even on my most difficult days, I rarely asked for help. When asked how I was doing, I always responded with, "I'm fine." I imagine you respond the same way when asked how you are, regardless of how you truly feel on the inside.

During those months I definitely was not fine. I was emotionally and physically exhausted. I needed help, but I didn't want to admit it to anyone, including myself, or to be a burden to family and friends. Mostly, I didn't want anyone's memories of Ron to be of the eighty-pound cancer-ridden man in the hospital bed in our living room. I wanted them to remember him as he would have wanted them to—a healthy, happy, loving, and kind man with a great smile and a sparkle in his eyes.

So I pretended everything was "fine." I didn't ask anyone to sit with Ron so I could take a shower or a nap. I didn't ask anyone to pick up toilet paper and milk from the store. I didn't ask for warm meals or help with my laundry.

I know there are many people in that same position for one reason or another, and, like me, they aren't asking for help. Maybe it's a caregiver. Maybe it's someone with a chronic illness, a sick family member, or someone experiencing the loss of a job.

They may not be asking, but the need is still there. Here are some practical ways you can reach out to those around you, whether they ask for help or not:

- Write a sweet note letting them know they are in your prayers and that you are there if they need you.

- Don't wait for them to ask for help. Just do something. Imagine yourself in their situation and think about what you would want someone to do for you. Then do it.
- Purchase some basic household items and deliver them. When you are going through something traumatic, it's hard to think about needing toilet paper, paper towels, tissues, drinks, etc. If their situation is one that brings lots of visitors, they will need these items more than ever and rarely will anyone think to bring them.
- Make a casserole. I'm a Southern girl, and the go-to dish for any need is a casserole. Casseroles feed a good crowd, are warm and comforting, and can easily be frozen in case others had the same idea.
- Bring dinner to a shut-in and stay to share the meal.
- Run errands or do yard work for someone who is unable to take care of these things for him- or herself.
- Call your local shelter and ask if they need help serving food or need blankets or other items.
- Send cards to troops overseas or help the family of a soldier who is overseas. I bet they would love phone cards!
- Visit children in the chronically ill ward of the hospital. Family members need time to spend at home with their other children, and this provides them with a much-needed break. You can read to the kids or play board games or color with them.
- Welcome a new family with a basket of baked goodies. If they are new to the town, include local maps, menus to your favorite restaurants, and information on the area you think would be helpful or interesting.
- Invite a widow, a widower, a foreign exchange student from a local college, or a lonely teen over to share Sunday dinner or to join your family for a holiday or special occasion.

If all those years ago I had understood that helping blesses the giver as much as the receiver, I might have accepted the help I needed. If I had known the joy one feels when making a casserole for someone in need, I might have admitted we were living on cereal.

Friends, I pray God will nudge your hearts and reveal ways to reach out to those around you. And I pray you will ask for help when you are the heart in need. Once you have experienced the joy of being a blessing by extending a helping hand, you will never rob another of experiencing this same joy.

# GATHERING IN

No matter what you've done for yourself or for humanity, if you can't look back on
having given love and attention to your own family, what have you really accomplished?
—LEE IACOCCA

When I was growing up, we sat down together at the dinner table every night. Everyone did. Kids played outside until they heard mom or dad call them to come in for dinner. Lifestyles have changed, and sadly, family mealtime seems to be heading for extinction. Between shuttling kids to science fairs, playdates, and dance classes, sometimes all we can manage is a quick trip to the drive-through window before heading home to put clothes in the dryer, feed the dog, and get the kids into bed. We are being pulled farther and farther away from the family table, and activities are pulling us in too many exhausting directions.

Statistics show eating dinner together as a family can have significant benefits. Children who eat with their families do measurably better in school, develop healthier eating habits, and have more confidence in themselves, which leads to smarter choices with their peers. Stronger family bonds, mutual respect, and a general consideration for each other are enhanced as a result of family mealtime.

Nothing compares to gathering around the kitchen table and simply being together to share what's going on in our hearts. But sometimes it's fun to make dinner an event. Here are some ideas for conversation starters and mealtime activities that will have everyone looking forward to family dinner:

- Have a "picnic" in the living room. Spread a blanket or tablecloth out on the floor. Eat off of paper products and serve typical picnic food.
- Eat by candlelight or use your fine china for an everyday meal, not just on a special occasion.
- Eat dinner backward. Start with the dessert and end with the appetizer.
- Each night at dinner ask everyone at the table to share their best and worst moments of the day.

- Let the kids set a unique table. They can make place mats, place cards, a centerpiece, and napkin rings.
- Have everyone speak with an accent during the meal.
- Put a selection of ingredients on the counter and have the whole family work together to make dinner using only those ingredients. To make things fair, have everyone choose a few of the items that will go on the counter.
- Have family devotions during dinner.
- Make a new mealtime tradition for a specific night of the week. Some ideas:

> Taco Tuesday
> Fondue Friday
> Family "Date" Night (rent a movie and eat dinner together while you watch the movie)
> Breakfast for Dinner Night
> Dippy Dinner (everything you serve comes with a dip)

- Go around the table, taking turns sharing where you saw God that day.
- Have a pajama party. Everyone puts on their silliest pajamas, eats pizza in front of the fireplace, plays Twister, and then eats popcorn while sharing silly stories.
- In the morning, select a country, state, or city that has been in the news. Announce the location and then, at dinner, everyone shares what they have discovered about the location.
- Place a jar or box of questions and topics on the table. Take turns pulling one out of the jar each night. Spend mealtime discussing what was chosen.
- Have everyone bring an interesting vocabulary word to the table. See if anyone knows what the words mean. Try to stump each other.

Play a word game during dinner! Here are a few that will have everyone laughing:

- Categories: Take turns saying a word in a chosen category (music, movies, food, ice-cream flavors, names of candy, cities, etc.) or words beginning with the same letter. For example, if the category is music, take turns listing music-related words, like *sing, note, drums, concert, song title,* etc.
- Alphabet Game: In alphabetical order, take turns listing items you would take with you on an imaginary trip to a silly location. Before listing an item, you have to

repeat the intro sentence and all the previous items. For example, it's your turn and the letter is *G*. You must say, "I am taking a trip to Timbuktu and I have to pack my suitcase. I will be bringing anchovies, batteries, a cow, doorknob, envelopes, football, and a _____ (your *G* word)." I have never made it all the way to *Z*!

- Tell a "Chain Story." One person begins to tell a creative story. After a couple of sentences, the story is "passed" to the person on the right, who continues with a few sentences and then passes to the next person on the right . . . The result will be some very interesting, creative, and silly storytelling.

Have theme days:

- Color of the day: Everyone wears and eats only items of that color.
- Food Item Day: Eat foods that are made from one food item. For example, if the food was an apple, you would eat things like apples, dried apples, baked apples, apple pie, applesauce, candy apples, biscuits with apple butter or apple jelly, apple-glazed chicken, and drink apple juice and spiced hot apple cider.
- Foreign Food Day: Choose one country and eat food from that region all day. For example, if you choose France, have crêpes Suzette or croissants for breakfast and coq au vin for dinner. You can turn this into a family educational experience by having each person research different things about the country to share during dinner.
- Instead of choosing a country, make up your own! Decide where your country is located, what foods they would eat, what the weather is like, what is the standard mode of transportation, what their words are for certain items, what the houses look like, etc. Create a menu to go with your country and let everyone help with the preparations.

I know it isn't realistic to think we can all gather around the kitchen table every night of the week. But remember the importance of family and the immeasurable benefits of eating together as often as possible. Reaching out with love should begin in our own home.

# HEARTFELT THANKS

My heart overflows when friends and family are gathered around my fingerprint-smudged dining room table. *The Loving Kitchen* is possible only because of you and the love you have shown me.

My mancub—They say home is where the heart is. Then you are mine. Remember that when I arrive on your doorstep with all my belongings in about thirty years.

Mom—You have given me a lifetime of love and support, and you still make me your tuna noodle casserole when I get nostalgic. Thank you for a childhood filled with home-cooked meals around the family table (except for the ones with lima beans). I am so lucky God chose you to be my mommy!

My family—Bob, Pat, Ron, Kris, John, Megan, Kelsie, Joe, Cinda, Haley, Brett, Pam, Rachael, and Brett Jr. Laughter shared over a meal brings me so much joy. I only wish we gathered around the kitchen table more often.

My friends, who are family—Vickie and Billy, Rhonda and Chris, Greg, Floyd and Dean, and Ken and Cindy. Words could never convey the depth of my love and appreciation for the grace, love, and support you have always extended. You are my safe place.

Ian—You tested most of the recipes that made it into this book, as well as the disasters that didn't. Not once did you complain, even when I made you cat capers. I love you for laughing every time I set off the smoke alarm. I love you even more for smiling and not saying a word when you bit into overcooked salmon, the Brussels sprouts I failed to conceal, and the chicken bones I accidentally left in the cacciatore. You make my heart smile.

Jackie and Gabriel, the precious ones—I treasure every ooey gooey sticky finger treat-baking moment I get to spend with you. God's grace shines through the unconditional love you wrap in every hug, through every sweet prayer you lift up on my behalf, and through every, "I love you, LeLe." You melt my heart.

My Spirit of Joy family—You glorify God through your kindness, generosity, prayers, and support. My life was forever changed the moment I first walked through the door. The name on the sign may say Spirit of Joy. But it could just as easily read, "Spirit of God's Grace and Love."

My extraordinary blog readers—Y'all are the best! You have become treasured friends who bless me through your encouragement, TMI sharing, and photos of your own kitchen adventures. Thank you for pulling up a chair at my kitchen table.

My literary agent and dear friend, Jonathan Clements—When other agents were knocking on my door, you promised to always support me and represent me with integrity, but said your priority would always be to be home for dinner with your family whenever possible. That sealed the deal. You stuck with me when anyone else would have written me off, proving you are a man of your word. You are an honorable, godly man and truly a treasure in my life.

My Thomas Nelson family, especially my rockin' editor, Heather Skelton—Thank you from the bottom of my heart for your encouragement, wisdom, and humor, and for rearranging words, ketching my spellin errers, and making sure each page turned out so lovely. It doesn't seem right that your name is not alongside mine on the cover. This is "our" book.

And Ron—I thank God for the hope we have in Jesus. Because of Him, we will share a table again one day.

# INDEX

whipping cream, 199–200

    Dark Chocolate Strawberry Shortcake, 201

Whole Wheat Baked Penne with Vegetables, 131

Wild Rice Salad, 67

wraps, 89

## Z

zucchini

    Primavera Pasta Salad, 68

    roasted, 159

    Tequila Shrimp Skewers, 121

    Whole Wheat Baked Penne with Vegetables, 131

# ABOUT LEANN RICE

After several years living in the beautiful Pacific Northwest, LeAnn and her son, Nick, moved down south to sweet tea country for a fresh start after the death of her husband. The longer she lives in the South, the more her tongue seems to curl as she speaks, and the more "y'all," "I reckon" and "bless their hearts" slip from her lips, much to the amusement of family back in Washington State.

She is passionate about sharing grace with others through preparing and serving delicious down-home food with warmth, humor, and unmistakable Southern charm and hospitality. LeAnn's heart is in welcoming the neighbor, nurturing the family, and bringing people around the kitchen table to share good food, laughter, and treasured conversations while creating lasting memories.

LeAnn reaches tens of thousands through her popular food blog, www.LeAnnCooks.org, a site she developed to share recipes, glimpses into her life and the more than occasional kitchen disaster. When she's not blogging, going to the theater, packing a care package for her now college-age son, or trying to appease their high-maintenance cat's unreasonable demands, you will find LeAnn creating new recipes to try out on brave friends who don't let an occasional oven fire frighten them off! She doesn't strive for perfection, and has been known to laugh, grab a fork, and sit down in the middle of the kitchen when a whole cheesecake falls to the floor.

At the end of the day it doesn't matter if there are still dirty dishes in her sink or if she ran out of time to update her Facebook page. What matters most is that her son knows he is loved unconditionally and that she didn't turn her back on a friend or someone in need of a warm bowl of comfort or a seat at her table.